Baby-Led Weaning

Made Easy

Baby-Led Weaning
Made Easy

The Busy Parent's Guide to
Feeding Babies *and* Toddlers
with Delicious Family Meals

Simone Ward

Creator of **ZAYNE'S PLATE**

PHOTOGRAPHY BY BECKY WINKLER

PAGE STREET
PUBLISHING CO.

Copyright © 2021 Simone Ward

First published in 2021 by
Page Street Publishing Co.
27 Congress Street, Suite 105
Salem, MA 01970
www.pagestreetpublishing.com

Distributed by Macmillan, sales in Canada by The Canadian Manda Group.

25   24   23   22   21   1 2 3 4 5

ISBN-13: 978-1-64567-227-2
ISBN-10: 1-64567-227-1

Library of Congress Control Number: 2020945236

Cover and book design by Rosie Stewart for Page Street Publishing Co.
Photography by Becky Winkler

Printed and bound in the United States of America

DEDICATION

TO MY DARLING CHILDREN, ASHER, CARYS, BAY AND ZAYNE. WITHOUT YOU, NONE OF THIS WOULD BE POSSIBLE. I LOVE YOU ALWAYS AND FOREVER.

Contents

CHAPTER 3
Twenty-Minute Meals   75

CHAPTER 4
One-Pot and Sheet-Pan Meals   97

CHAPTER 5
Slow Cooker and Instant Pot® Meals   119

Foreword

Feeding babies can be hard! After helping thousands of parents from around the world with feeding their children, I can't tell you how many times I hear this. Whether they are unsure about how to start solid foods, how to help their child learn to like new foods or how to help their baby eat what the rest of the family does, all parents have their own struggles when it comes to meals.

No matter their struggles, though, one of the most common requests I get from parents is for more recipes that are baby friendly. How to introduce new textures, flavors and culinary experiences to their children is always at the top of parents' lists. And that is where Simone comes in!

When I first discovered Simone and her Instagram account a few years ago, I was impressed by the creativity behind the meals she shared. They were not just visually pleasing and clearly nutritious; they were realistic and things that I could see myself making. Because at the end of a busy day, I'm all about making quick and nutritious meals that don't take me hours and hours in the kitchen.

As a mother of four, Simone has a confident handle on quick, easy and creative meals. She knows how to get to the heart of recipes and doesn't bother with steps that keep you in the kitchen for an endless amount of time. But with that said, her recipes have always been ones that actually make you want to get in the kitchen—recipes that promise tons of flavor, without all the work.

I'm so excited that Simone has decided to funnel her culinary creativity into a cookbook. The recipes here are full of flavor, nutritious and—above all—easy. No need to be an expert chef to make your family delicious meals. Because as much as this cookbook is about baby-led weaning and full of baby-friendly recipes, it's family friendly too!

The beautiful thing about baby-led weaning is that your baby generally eats what you do. The recipes in this book have all been created with your baby in mind, though. They are safe from choking hazards and prioritize your baby's nutritional needs. But don't be fooled. These are recipes that will become family favorites and go-to meals for your whole family.

Simone has an excellent understanding of how to make recipes for babies as nutritious as possible. There are certain nutrients, like iron, that we need to focus on to help our babies get what they need to thrive. With the recipes in this cookbook, Simone is placing an emphasis on iron sources and other nutrient-dense foods, which makes my dietitian heart happy! And for many of those recipes that are not iron-rich themselves, Simone gives some suggestions to help you round out the meal or snack. A book like this—full of nutritious and safe recipes—is a great help for parents to ensure their baby is getting exactly what they need.

So if you're ready to dive into some quick, easy and nutritious recipes for your baby and whole family, pull up a chair and grab a cup of tea. This book is truly a gem for your baby and your family as a whole!

—RENAE D'ANDREA, MS, RDN
Baby-led weaning and toddler registered dietitian

Introduction

Welcome! I'm Simone, a busy mom of four, all of whom were weaned onto solids using the baby-led weaning method. I run a popular Instagram blog where I have helped thousands of parents increase the variety in their kids' diets, as well as gain the confidence to introduce new foods in simple and realistic ways. In the last few years, I have worked extensively in recipe development, both domestically and internationally, and it is truly an honor to be able share my experiences, ideas and recipes with you in my first cookbook.

If there's one thing I am passionate about, it's helping babies and toddlers discover the joys of taste and food exploration with nutritious and balanced meals. I am a huge advocate of introducing babies to a wide variety of foods as early as possible, and that's because research has shown that the early introduction of different foods and flavors can help diversify your baby's palate and support them in becoming adventurous eaters later in life. I believe that the most practical way to achieve this is by creating family-centered meals that can be easily adapted for your baby to eat.

I know all too well the challenges that can arise when putting baby-led weaning into practice, especially when life gets busy and it feels like there just isn't enough time to get a home-cooked, nutritious and well-balanced plate of food on the table. This conundrum is why I wanted to create a baby-led weaning cookbook with the busy parent in mind—one that simplifies the way we make meals to make life easier and support you through feeding both your baby and toddler, as well as your family as a whole. If you want to cook hearty homemade meals the easy way, you are in the right place!

Working closely with Renae D'Andrea, a pediatric dietitian nutritionist who specializes in baby-led weaning, I have broken down the process to get right to the heart of the approach and provide only the necessary information so that you can safely and effectively wean your baby onto solids. What's more, each and every recipe and meal recommendation is suitable from 6 months of age and has been approved as nutritionally balanced and safe for your baby to eat. So you can rest assured that all of the advice, information, recipes and meal ideas in this book are high quality, in line with current guidelines and backed by up-to-date, evidence-based research.

Not only do I provide you with nutritionally well-rounded recipes and meal ideas, I also walk you through some of the ways that you can reduce your cooking-related stress and manage your time more effectively by taking shortcuts where needed to find a balance that fits your lifestyle. And while the recipes are designed to keep mealtimes simple, they do not compromise on flavor or texture. This is not a cookbook of fancy finger foods just for your baby—this is a cookbook of delicious recipes that will appeal to everyone in your family.

I would like to take this opportunity to wish you well on your and your baby's weaning journey, and I hope that this cookbook will not only give you a variety of delicious, baby-friendly recipes but also a good understanding of how to build simple meals that are well rounded and nutritious. In a time when nutrition can often seem so complicated, I hope that you will see that proper nutrition doesn't have to be that way in everyday life. With all the modern time constraints that we parents face, keeping things simple and manageable is the easiest way to approach the minefield that is feeding our children. So pop your baby down for a nap, put your feet up, pour yourself a cup of tea and let us begin this journey of feeding your baby wholesome and tasty meals!

Simone Ward

A QUICK GUIDE to Baby-Led Weaning

Baby-led weaning (or BLW) is a strategy for introducing solids that has gained huge popularity in the past few years. Originally coined by former midwife Gill Rapley, the basic principle behind baby-led weaning is to skip spoon-feeding your baby purees and instead offer appropriately prepared finger foods and family-style meals.

The idea of skipping purees and allowing baby to self-feed appeals to a lot of families, and not just because of the developmental benefits but also because it can save time—and for many of us time is very much of the essence!

It is common to be anxious about introducing solids, but I want you to know that baby-led weaning is a very safe and simple weaning method. One of its main benefits is that it can easily be worked into your family's life. In this chapter, I will walk you through the basics of baby-led weaning and how to get started, how to build nutritious and balanced plates and how to safely serve foods in line with your baby's development.

Getting Started

SIGNS OF READINESS

It is recommended that your baby starts solids when they are showing signs of readiness, which typically happens at about 6 months of age. Your baby may show these signs a little earlier or later than 6 months, which is okay, as most babies will become developmentally ready in their own time.

If you decide to introduce solids before 6 months, it is important to wait until your baby is at least 4 months (17 weeks) old. Prior to this age, their digestive tract is not developed enough to handle solid foods.

Signs of readiness include the following:

✓ Baby can sit up unaided without support for at least 5 seconds (see Nutritionist's Tip)

✓ Baby has lost their tongue-thrust reflex and doesn't thrust their tongue out when something like a spoon is brought to their mouth

✓ Baby has developed some hand-to-eye coordination as well as sufficient palm grasping so that they can pick up food and put it in their mouth

✓ Baby shows an interest in food

NUTRITIONIST'S TIP: Sitting up unaided is the number one sign we look for when it comes to starting solids, especially with BLW. When babies are not sitting up for at least a few seconds, they do not have proper core control to eat safely and prevent choking. So make sure that your baby is sitting before starting BLW!

WHAT YOU WILL NEED

When it comes to BLW, you won't need much. Here are my recommendations for the essentials to get you started.

HIGH CHAIR

The high chair is the most important piece of equipment you will need. Ensuring that your baby's seated position is stable and comfortable is key to successful mealtimes.

Here are the features you should look for in a high chair:

✓ An adjustable footrest that provides stability and ensures that your baby's knees are at a 90-degree angle

✓ A seat that doesn't slouch backward and allows your baby to sit with their hips at a 90-degree angle

✓ It is also helpful (but not essential) if it has a detachable tray to allow your baby to join the table during mealtimes.

GOOD TO KNOW: If you already have a high chair and it doesn't have a footrest, try propping a chair or a stool under your baby's feet instead. There are also many safe modifications for popular high chairs available to purchase online at reasonable prices, so be sure to check those out for a more permanent solution.

Travel high chairs (or high chairs provided at restaurants) do not need to meet the same requirements as your main high chair, as they will only be used occasionally and for short periods of time. All that is required for those situations is that your baby can be strapped in safely and that the chairs are functional—anything else is a bonus but not essential!

HERE IS A LIST OF OTHER ITEMS YOU WILL NEED:

✓ Smash-proof tableware—at least two bowls and two plates

✓ Three to five baby-friendly spoons with short, easy-to-grip handles

✓ Three to five full-sleeved or smock bibs

✓ A cup—avoid spouted sippy cups and beakers, as they may interfere with muscle and speech development. Instead, opt for a small open-top cup, a straw cup or a leakproof training cup.

- ✓ A large sheet or drop cloth or a large wipe-clean mat to place under the high chair

- ✓ Durable lunchbox for eating on the go

- ✓ Crinkle-shaped food cutter to make slippery foods easier to handle

- ✓ Small popsicle molds with easy-to-hold handles

FIRST FOODS

It may be tempting to just place a random plate of food in front of your baby and let them go at it. While this can be absolutely fine—and fun to watch!—we do need to give some thought to what is on that plate.

NUTRITION

Your baby's nutritional needs begin to change and will become more demanding at about 6 months of age. Most of these needs, such as calcium, protein, choline and vitamin C, will be met through breastmilk or formula. However, breastmilk is low in iron, which can be problematic as your baby's iron stores begin to deplete around this time. Because iron and zinc play a vital role in your baby's health, growth and development, we need to pay special attention to offering foods that are iron-rich regardless of whether your baby is breastfed or formula-fed.

This doesn't mean that you need to set aside extra time to make separate special meals for your baby. Instead, you can focus on including iron-rich foods in your family meals and serve your baby a few appropriately prepared pieces of food from each meal. You should aim to include one iron-rich food in every meal that you serve your baby.

In addition, aim to make your baby's diet as varied as possible by including a variety of carbohydrates, healthy fats, fruits, vegetables, legumes and pulses and, if you wish, eggs, dairy, fish and meat. This variety will help ensure that your baby is exposed to a wide range of nutrients as well as support their sensory and oral development.

MEAL BUILDING

One of the simplest and most effective ways to build a balanced plate for your baby is one that is recommended by BLW expert Renae D'Andrea, whereby you ensure that each meal you serve your baby contains

- ✓ an iron-rich food;

- ✓ a high-calorie food; and

- ✓ a fruit and/or vegetable.

It is no longer advised to introduce individual foods to your baby one at a time, so feel free to offer plates with all three food groups right from the beginning. With that said, try not to overwhelm your baby with a large amount of food all at once—it's best to serve only a few pieces of food at a time and top up their plate as needed.

SIMPLE MEAL-BUILDING EXAMPLES

In the tables that follow, you will find ideas for nutritionally balanced plates for babies 6+ months and also for 8 to 9+ months. I've included recipes from this book so you can see a practical application for everyday life. But please do not feel like you have to follow this as a meal plan by cooking and baking everything from scratch each day—that would certainly be ambitious! Simply come to this list whenever you are feeling stuck in a rut for what to make and use it for inspiration.

Note that "freezer stash" foods should be thawed before serving.

6+ MONTHS		
BREAKFAST IDEAS	**LUNCH IDEAS**	**DINNER IDEAS**
Iron-Rich: Fried egg with a hard yolk, cut into strips **High-Calorie + Fruit:** Mashed banana on whole-grain toast, cut into strips	**Iron-Rich + High-Calorie + Vegetable:** Freezer stash or fresh Sweet Potato and Broccoli Tots (page 33) and tahini, tots served whole with tahini spread on top	**Iron-Rich + High-Calorie + Vegetable:** Sheet-Pan Mediterranean Salmon (page 116), salmon flaked and potatoes and veggies served as they are
Iron-Rich + High-Calorie: Greek yogurt spread onto freezer stash or fresh Peanut Butter Banana Bread (page 30), cut into strips **Fruit:** Soft strawberries, served whole if large or quartered if small	**High-Calorie + Fruit:** Mashed avocado spread onto whole-grain bagel, sliced through the middle and halved **Iron-Rich:** Hard-boiled egg, quartered	**Iron-Rich + High-Calorie:** Spinach and Almond Pesto Pasta (page 82) **Vegetable:** Grape or cherry tomatoes, quartered lengthwise
Iron-Rich + High-Calorie: Greek yogurt mixed with nut butter of choice or up to 2 tablespoons (30 g) Chia Jam (page 69), preloaded onto spoons or served in a bowl **Fruit:** Ripe pear, cored and cut into strips	**Iron-Rich:** Freezer stash or fresh Mixed Bean Burgers (page 73), cut into strips **High-Calorie + Vegetable:** Buttered corn on the cob	**Iron-Rich + Vegetable:** Sheet-Pan Chicken Fajitas (page 104), served as they are **High-Calorie:** Tortilla wrap, cut into strips
Iron-Rich + High-Calorie + Vegetable: Carrot Cake Steel-Cut Oatmeal (page 121), preloaded onto spoons or served in a bowl	**Iron-Rich + High-Calorie:** Herby Hummus Dip (page 70) spread onto pita bread or toast, cut into strips **Fruit:** Watermelon, seeds removed and cut into sticks	**Iron-Rich + High-Calorie + Vegetable:** Steak and Potato Dinner Hash (page 103), steak cut into strips and potatoes and veggies served as they are
Iron-Rich + High-Calorie + Fruit: Peanut butter and banana tortilla wrap, sliced	**Iron-Rich + Vegetable:** Freezer stash or fresh Salmon and Pea Egg Muffins (page 39), cut in half or quartered **High-Calorie:** Buttered toast, cut into strips	**Iron-Rich + High-Calorie + Vegetable:** Cheats Veggie Pizza (page 81), cut into strips

BREAKFAST IDEAS	LUNCH IDEAS	DINNER IDEAS
Iron-Rich: Freezer stash or fresh Lemon and Raspberry Oat Cups (page 62), whole, halved or quartered **High-Calorie:** Greek yogurt, dolloped onto oat cups, preloaded onto spoons or served in a bowl **Fruit:** Baked apple slices	**Iron-Rich + High-Calorie + Vegetable:** Freezer stash or fresh Veggie-Loaded Quiche (page 66), cut into bite-sized pieces **Fruit:** Ripe pear, cored and cut into bite-sized pieces	**Iron-Rich:** Lentil Bolognese (page 143) **High-Calorie:** Spaghetti, snipped with scissors or chopped with a knife **Vegetable:** Steamed or roasted green beans, cut into bite-sized pieces
Iron-Rich + High-Calorie: Peanut Butter and Jam Overnight Oats (page 69), preloaded onto spoons or served in a bowl **Fruit:** Banana, cut into bite-sized pieces	**Iron-Rich:** Chickpea or lentil pasta **High-Calorie:** Cheese sauce **Vegetable:** Roasted or steamed broccoli, whole florets (if small) or cut into bite-sized pieces	**Iron-Rich + High-Calorie:** Avocado, Black Bean and Mozzarella Quesadillas (page 94), cut into strips **Vegetable:** Fresh salsa, for dipping
Iron-Rich: Freezer stash or fresh Vanilla Oat Waffles (page 35), cut into bite-sized pieces **High-Calorie:** Whipped cream or Greek yogurt, spread onto waffles or served as a dip **Fruit:** Fresh or thawed frozen blueberries, squished or halved	**Iron-Rich + Vegetable:** Freezer stash or fresh Spiced Carrot and Lentil Fritters (page 29), cut into bite-sized pieces **High-Calorie:** Avocado, cut into bite-sized pieces	**Iron-Rich + High-Calorie + Vegetable:** Mexican Chicken and Rice (page 111), chicken cut into bite-sized pieces
Iron-Rich: 2 tablespoons (30 g) Coconut Chia Pudding (page 65; see Nutritionist's Tip on the next page), preloaded onto spoons **High-Calorie:** French toast, cut into strips or bite-sized pieces **Fruit:** Fresh mango, cut into bite-sized pieces	**Iron-Rich + High-Calorie:** Hummus (homemade or store-bought) and mushroom toast, cut into strips **Fruit:** Kiwi, peeled and sliced or cut into bite-sized pieces	**Iron-Rich:** Baby-Friendly Chicken Curry (page 125), served as is **High-Calorie:** Sticky rice, served as is or rolled into balls **Vegetable:** Steamed or roasted carrots, cut into bite-sized pieces

NUTRITIONIST'S TIP: Avoid offering overly thick chia pudding on a spoon or in a bowl, as it may become globby, making it hard to swallow. Instead, opt for a runnier consistency when serving it this way.

A NOTE ON SERVING SIZES

Since babies' and toddlers' appetites vary, the child serving suggestions that I give in the recipes are more of a guide rather than a rule and will often allow for your baby or toddler to have seconds or thirds if desired.

I recommend starting with small portions and topping up your baby or toddler's plate as needed. This will help to prevent your baby or toddler from becoming overwhelmed during mealtimes, as well as reduce food waste.

By serving meals this way, you may find that you often have leftovers, which will be an added bonus and will help you build up your refrigerator and freezer stash for quick and easy meals throughout the days and weeks.

Also note that some recipes include volume amounts that you may find helpful when deciding how much you will need for your family, or if you are making them ahead or perhaps solely for your baby or toddler and want to portion the servings out ahead of time.

Be aware that the amount of food shown in the images accompanying the recipes are not intended as portion size guidance. Please adapt portion sizes according to your baby's age and appetite. As mentioned above, it's better to start with a small amount and top up if they would like more.

INTRODUCING ALLERGENS

It wasn't that long ago that we were advised to avoid offering babies allergenic foods during the first year. We now know that in order to reduce the risk of babies developing food allergies, allergenic foods should be offered alongside other foods while we are introducing solids. We also know that consistent exposure to allergenic foods may further reduce the risk of developing allergies. In short, it's okay to offer allergenic foods from six months onward, and you should offer them often!

When introducing allergens for the first time, I do recommend offering them one at a time alongside nonallergenic foods. This is so that if your baby does have an allergic reaction, you can be certain which allergen was the culprit. Once you have established that no allergy is present, you can combine allergenic foods in a meal if desired.

Top allergens are as follows:

✓ Dairy, such as milk, cream, butter, cheese and yogurt

✓ Eggs

✓ Soy

✓ Peanuts and tree nuts, such as almonds, cashews, hazelnuts, pecans, pine nuts and pistachios

✓ Wheat

✓ Fish

✓ Shellfish

MEAL FREQUENCY

At the beginning of starting solids, you may find it challenging to incorporate meals and snacks into your baby's routine. With this in mind, I recommend starting with one to two meals per day, with the aim of building up to three meals per day by 12 months and introducing snacks thereafter. You can work your way up to this by using the following guide.

AGE	MEAL FREQUENCY PER DAY
6 months	1 to 2 meals
9 months	3 meals
12 months	3 meals + 2 snacks

Remember, each baby will be different: For some, introducing more meals and snacks earlier will be preferred, whereas others may take longer to increase their solids intake. Follow your baby's lead and use this as a guide only.

MILK FEEDS

It can be tricky figuring how to incorporate milk feeds alongside solids. The most important thing to keep in mind is that up until 12 months, breastmilk and/or formula will continue to be your baby's main source of nutrients and calories. This is not to say that solid foods are not important, but they should not replace milk feeds in their entirety. I recommend offering a milk feed 30 to 60 minutes before serving solid foods. It is also important that babies should still be fed breastmilk and/or formula on demand for the first year. I talk more about toddlers and milk consumption in the "Common Questions" section (page 24) at the end of this chapter.

How to Serve Foods

When it comes to BLW, there is a general consensus that pretty much anything goes—and yes, it is true that this method allows for a lot of freedom around self-feeding, but there are some things that need to be considered to ensure that your baby eats safely and in line with their development.

SIZE, SHAPE AND TEXTURE

SIZE AND SHAPE FOR 6 TO 8 MONTHS

At about 6 months, your baby will likely pick things up by grasping them with their whole palm. To make it easier for them to pick up food and eat it, it is best to cut foods—where possible—into long strips roughly the length and width of one to two adult fingers. Not all foods can be cut to this size and that is okay—you should still serve them, being sure to cut any round foods in halves or quarters.

The image on the next page shows some examples of how to prepare various foods for babies 6 to 8 months of age.

SIZE AND SHAPE FOR 8 TO 9+ MONTHS

As your baby grows, they will further develop the ability to pick up smaller pieces of food with their thumb and index finger. This is called the pincer grasp, and it is at this point that you can start to cut food into smaller pieces. Cutting food into smaller pieces encourages your baby to strengthen their pincer grasp, which is important for the development of fine motor skills. But remember that you can still include stick-shaped foods in their meals too—it doesn't have to be all of one and none of the other!

The image on page 20 shows some examples of how to prepare various foods for babies 8 to 9+ months of age.

TEXTURE

In the early days and weeks, it is best to serve foods that are soft enough to be squished between two fingers. Make sure that any hard fruits and vegetables are steamed, roasted or stewed and that cooked meats are moist and tender.

As your baby grows and further practices their chewing skills, you can begin to introduce al dente textures. These include foods such as raw bell peppers (served any way you or your baby prefers), grated raw carrots and grated raw apples—pretty much anything that isn't a choking hazard. I talk more about choking hazards starting on page 22.

EXAMPLES OF FOODS APPROPRIATE FOR 6 TO 8 MONTHS

BANANAS
Half of a banana with the peel cut from the top and the bottom portion of peel left intact for a handle, or sliced in quarters lengthwise

CUCUMBERS
Cut into sticks approximately the length and width of one adult finger, with or without skin

COOKED STEAK
Cut into thin strips

STEAMED, BAKED OR SAUTÉED APPLES
Peeled, cored and sliced into wedges or sticks

GRAPES
Quartered lengthwise

BUTTERED TOAST
Cut into strips approximately the length and width of one to two adult fingers, with or without crust

STEAMED OR ROASTED BROCCOLI
Whole florets

HARD-BOILED EGGS
Quartered lengthwise

RIPE AVOCADOS
Cut into wedges approximately the width of one adult finger, with skin (as pictured) or without skin

RIPE STRAWBERRIES
Whole if large and quartered if small

CHERRY TOMATOES
Quartered lengthwise

STEAMED OR ROASTED CARROTS
Cut into sticks approximately the length and width of one adult finger

CHEESE
Grated

STEAMED OR ROASTED CAULIFLOWER
Whole florets

BOILED PASTA
Fusilli or rigatoni, whole and cooked until tender

BLUEBERRIES
Squished, mashed or halved if small and quartered if large

EXAMPLES OF FOODS APPROPRIATE FOR 8 TO 9+ MONTHS

BANANAS
Diced into small pieces

CUCUMBERS
Diced into medium pieces, without skin

COOKED STEAK
Diced into small pieces

STEAMED, BAKED OR SAUTÉED APPLES
Cut into bite-sized pieces

GRAPES
Quartered lengthwise

BUTTERED TOAST
Cut into bite-sized pieces, with or without crust

STEAMED OR ROASTED BROCCOLI
Florets cut into bite-sized pieces

HARD-BOILED EGGS
Cut into bite-sized pieces

RIPE AVOCADOS
Diced into medium pieces

RIPE STRAWBERRIES
Quartered or diced into medium pieces

CHERRY TOMATOES
Quartered lengthwise

STEAMED OR ROASTED CARROTS
Diced into small pieces

CHEESE
Grated or diced into small pieces

STEAMED OR ROASTED CAULIFLOWER
Florets cut into bite-sized pieces

BOILED PASTA
Elbow, macaroni or small shells

BLUEBERRIES
Squished, mashed or halved if small and quartered if large

SLIPPERY FOODS

Some foods can be slippery and may be difficult for your baby to pick up and hold. To help with this, you can use a crinkle cutter to cut foods, or you can try rolling slippery foods such as avocado, banana, mango or kiwi in ground flaxseed, ground almonds, breadcrumbs or unsweetened desiccated coconut. If the food you are serving has a skin, you can also try leaving some of it on the bottom of the piece food for your child to grip, but do ensure that you are watching your baby at all times so that you can take away the skins once they have finished eating.

SERVING TIP: Make bananas less slippery by sliding your finger lengthwise into the center of a peeled banana until it splits into three long pieces, and then break those pieces in half. These individual pieces will be much easier for your baby to pick up and eat.

TEETH—OR LACK THEREOF!

Something that often surprises people is that babies do not need to have teeth to chew firmer foods, as they have incredibly hard gums. My eldest child didn't cut his first tooth until he was 13 months old, and in that time, he was chomping down on all manner of foods—including steak!

When you think about it, we chew and grind down food with our molars and not our front teeth. If you were to wait until your baby cut their molars at 1 or 2 years old to offer different and more challenging textures, they would miss out on a crucial opportunity to explore, learn and develop food preferences.

Safety

The risk of choking is without a doubt one of the biggest worries parents have when offering solid foods, particularly so with BLW or the introduction of finger foods alongside purees. The good news is that choking is rare, and there are many things you can do to further reduce the risk of your baby choking.

FIRST AID

Before starting your baby on solids, I highly recommend taking a basic pediatric or infant first aid and CPR course so that you know what to do if your baby chokes. Not only can this save your baby's life, but it will also help reduce your anxiety and keep you calm and confident during mealtimes.

CREATING A SAFE FEEDING ENVIRONMENT

We tend to focus on the food itself when we think about the risks of choking, but creating a safe feeding environment for mealtimes is just as important.

Here is a checklist to help you create a safe feeding environment:

- ✓ Your baby is sitting up straight without slouching.

- ✓ Your baby is sitting securely in a high chair or booster seat that provides adequate back support.

- ✓ A responsible adult is present to supervise the meal and is watching the child at all times.

- ✓ The television is off and all electronic devices are put away.

- ✓ For younger babies, finger foods should be soft enough to be squished between two adult fingers.

- ✓ Any choking hazards are modified (see the following section).

CHOKING HAZARDS AND SAFE MODIFICATIONS FOR CHILDREN YOUNGER THAN 4 YEARS OLD	
CHOKING HAZARD	SAFE MODIFICATION
Whole cherry or grape tomatoes	Quarter lengthwise
Whole grapes	Quarter lengthwise
Whole blueberries	Cut in half or squish
Raw carrots, apples and celery	Steam or bake until soft; for toddlers older than 12 months, you can also peel and shred raw items
Whole nuts and seeds	Finely chop or grind
Chunks or spoonfuls of nut butter	Spread thinly on foods or stir into yogurt, oatmeal or other pureed textures
Sausages and hot dogs	Slice into quarters lengthwise or chop into bite-sized pieces
String cheese or large chunks of hard cheese	Slice lengthwise or chop into bite-sized pieces
Large chunks of meat or strips of tough, dry meat	Cut into bite-sized pieces

CHOKING HAZARDS

Some foods need to be prepared in a specific way to minimize the risk of choking. In the table above, I have listed the top choking hazards and how you can make them safer for your baby.

Be aware that there are some foods to avoid completely until your child is at least 4 years old:

✓ Whole-kernel popcorn

✓ Hard chips, crisps and crackers

✓ Hard candy or sweets

✓ Marshmallows

✓ Chewing gum

Please note that this list is not extensive. Please refer to current government guidelines for a comprehensive list.

CHOKING VERSUS GAGGING

Understanding the difference between choking and gagging is very important so that you know when it is appropriate to intervene. It is often the case that parents mistake gagging, which is normal and a part of learning to eat, for choking, which is rare but serious.

GAGGING

When your baby is younger, their gag reflex is closer to the front of their mouth. Thus, they have a very strong gag reflex. This heightened gag reflex acts as a built-in safety mechanism designed to keep your baby safe from choking. You may find that your baby gags or retches often when eating, and while this can be unsettling and uncomfortable to watch, it is a very normal part of the learning process. It will improve over time and is nothing to be alarmed about.

The best course of action to take when your baby is gagging is to remain calm and allow them to work through the gag themselves, so that they can safely get the food to the front of their mouth. Do not intervene by sticking your fingers into your baby's mouth or slapping your baby's back. Unnecessary intervention may actually cause a baby to choke when they would not have otherwise.

Gagging involves the following signs:

- ✓ The child's face turns red and their eyes may close and/or water.

- ✓ The child may cough and/or retch, which can sometimes lead to vomiting.

- ✓ The child will open their mouth and thrust their tongue forward.

CHOKING

Actual choking is wholly different from gagging and occurs when food moves beyond your baby's gag reflex and completely or partially blocks their airway. When this happens, your baby will be unable to breathe and you must immediately begin using standard first aid.

Choking involves the following signs:

- ✓ The child's face and/or lips turn blue.

- ✓ Choking is usually silent, although a weak cough or gasp may be attempted.

- ✓ The child may begin to lose consciousness.

Foods to Avoid

While for the most part babies can eat what we eat, there are some foods that should be given sparingly or not given at all.

HONEY

Neither cooked nor raw honey should be given to babies younger than 1 year old due to the risk of botulism. Be aware that honey is often added to many prepared foods, such as flavored nut butters, granola bars, smoothies and even breads. Always check labels carefully.

EXCESS SALT

Babies and toddlers need only a small amount of salt in their diets. This is particularly important for babies younger than 1 year old, as they have immature kidneys that cannot cope with excess salt intake.

With this in mind, avoid offering your baby or toddler foods that are high in salt, and do not add salt to foods when cooking for your baby. You can always remove your baby's portion before salting the family meal—this is what I typically suggest for the recipes in this book.

CURRENT FDA/NHS SODIUM GUIDELINES		
AGE	SODIUM (MAX PER DAY)	SALT (MAX PER DAY)
Babies (younger than 12 months old)	400 mg	1 g
Toddlers (1 to 3 years old)	800 mg	2 g

ADDED SUGARS

For children younger than 2 years old, it is recommended that we should avoid serving foods with added sugar. This includes natural sugars such as pure maple syrup, honey and agave syrup. But it does not include fruits—pureed or otherwise—which are perfectly fine to use as sweeteners.

Chances are your baby or toddler will have the occasional food with added sugar before they are 2 years old, and that is absolutely fine—it won't hurt them! It's just something to be mindful of when thinking about the foods we choose to serve and making simple swaps where we can.

Within the recipes in this book, the instruction to add natural sugars is optional, and I only recommended this for children 2 years and older.

LIGHTLY COOKED OR RAW EGGS

Eggs must be fully cooked for children younger than 5 years old, with the exception of eggs that are pasteurized.

RAW FISH AND MEDIUM-RARE MEATS

Do not offer children younger than 5 years old raw or partially cooked fish, such as sushi. Ensure that meats, such as poultry and pork, are fully cooked. Red meats, such as steak and lamb, can be offered slightly pink in the middle as long as the internal temperature reaches 145°F (63°C) on a meat thermometer during cooking.

Common Questions

IS IT SAFE TO COMBINE FINGER FOODS AND SPOON-FEEDING?

Absolutely! There is no evidence to suggest that combining spoon-feeding purees with finger foods is dangerous; in fact, it is advisable for traditional weaning that you offer appropriately prepared finger foods alongside purees right from the beginning of starting solids. With that said, by the time your baby reaches 11 months of age, they should be eating primarily finger foods irrespective of your chosen feeding method.

MY BABY IS MOSTLY PLAYING WITH THEIR FOOD INSTEAD OF EATING IT. SHOULD I BE WORRIED?

A lot of babies eat little during the first few weeks of BLW, which is very common and totally normal. Babies often spend more time exploring, touching, licking, smelling and playing with food than they do actually eating it, and this is all part of the learning process. Yes, some babies take to the eating part quickly, but many are cautious and take their sweet time before they become enthusiastic about solids. This doesn't mean that your baby is not a "good" eater, or that they are picky or not getting the hang of things. They are simply developing at their own pace.

Be sure to keep an eye on the contents of their diaper, as you may be surprised that they are in fact swallowing more food than you realize!

WHAT IS THE RIGHT PORTION SIZE FOR MY BABY?

There is no universal or "right" portion size when it comes to feeding babies and toddlers. How much food your child eats will depend on many different factors, such as growth spurts, teething or illness. Food intake will fluctuate from day to day and even meal to meal. One of the most unhelpful things we can do is compare our child's food intake with others, because how much a child eats will be individual to them and their needs. With that said, many babies and toddlers may become overwhelmed with larger portions of food and respond better when they are given smaller portions. Simply refill your baby's plate if they are still hungry.

SHOULD I GIVE MY BABY WATER?

Before 12 months of age, it is okay to offer your baby small amounts of water during meals to help them to wash down food, but outside of mealtimes you should only offer breastmilk and/or formula as a drink. After 12 months, you can offer water throughout the day as needed.

ALLOWING MY CHILD TO SELF-FEED IS SO MESSY! ARE THERE WAYS TO AVOID SO MUCH CLEANUP EVERY TIME?

I'm not going to beat around the bush here—baby-led weaning is going to be messy, and there is only so much we can do about it. Letting your baby take the lead in self-feeding means there will be lots of opportunities for them to learn, play and explore, and this will be done by smelling, touching squeezing, squelching, spreading, poking, throwing and—most satisfying of all—tasting the foods you serve. As challenging as this can be, one of the best ways to approach mess is to embrace it and remember that first, the mess is a good thing: Your baby is harnessing their curiosity and learning a lifelong skill. And second, remember that this too shall pass! Believe it or not, the messiness is not a particularly long phase, and as your baby gets the hang of eating, they will make less of a mess.

With that said, here are some things you can do to make cleanup a little easier and quicker:

✓ Get an easy-to-clean high chair with a removable tray. Avoid high chairs with fabric seams and cushioned covers, as they can quickly become grimy and will need to be removed and washed often.

✓ Save your floors by placing a large wipe-clean mat underneath the high chair.

✓ Invest in at least three full-sleeved smock bibs (preferably with a food catcher) to keep your baby's clothing clean. If you can find those super-large bibs that also cover baby's legs, even better!

✓ Let your baby go shirtless—this technique is especially handy if you plan on bathing them right after.

✓ Suction tableware helps keep plates and bowls stuck to the high chair tray or table and are a great option if you have a plate thrower, or if your baby instantly dumps their food out on the table. I find suction tableware particularly useful when serving soups. If possible, choose tableware with removable suction rings, so that they can grow with your baby.

✓ Avoid serving too much food on your baby's plate, as this may overwhelm your baby and actually encourage them to throw it on the floor. Instead, serve a few pieces at a time and top off as needed.

✓ Leave the cleaning until after your baby is completely finished eating. You may be tempted to clean up after them as they eat, but you'll only become frustrated, as they'll likely create the same mess again. Wait until they are finished and do a full sweep.

HOW MUCH MILK SHOULD MY TODDLER BE DRINKING?

From the age of 12 months, we start to approach milk intake differently than we did the first year. The focus now shifts onto solid foods as the primary source of nutrients and calories. If your toddler has transitioned to drinking animal- or plant-based milk, they should be offered no more than 16 ounces (480 ml) per day. This is because research has shown an increased risk of iron deficiency in toddlers who drink more milk than this. If your toddler is still breastfeeding, you can continue offering breastmilk on demand, so long as it doesn't interfere with baby's appetite for solid foods.

MAKE-AHEAD
Meals and Snacks

On my blog, I am always encouraging parents to make some of their family's meals and snacks ahead of time, so that they'll always have a good stock of quick and nutritious options on hand. I'm sure I sound like a broken record at times, but that's because batch-cooking and freezing is one of my most powerful weapons in what I like to call the battle against time.

Batch-cooking and freezing are what enable me to consistently provide my kids with a wide variety of nutritious foods, but without the stress and effort that often comes with day-to-day food prep and cooking. Batch-cooking and freezing will help make mealtimes a breeze and snack times a no-brainer! You will feel a sense of calm knowing that you have a freezer full of nutritious meal and snack options to quickly build tasty, balanced plates.

I talk more about the logistics of batch-cooking and freezing in "Bonus Time-Saving Tips" (page 147), where I go over the different ways you can work these techniques into your schedule as well as other ways you can prep foods in advance.

Spiced Carrot and Lentil Fritters

Fritters are one of the most practical foods for BLW. They are easy for babies to pick up and eat by themselves, and they can be made with a wide variety of nutritious foods. What's more, they taste delicious both hot and cold and are great for fuss-free, minimal-mess eating on the go. I don't think a week goes by without whipping up a batch of fritters for the freezer!

These gently spiced delights are crispy on the outside and soft on the inside and are a great way to introduce babies to the warm, earthy and slightly sweet flavors of turmeric and cumin. Adults will love these too—they pair brilliantly with a salad for a light-but-satisfying lunch.

1 cup (190 g) split red lentils

½ cup (55 g) grated carrots

2 scallions, thinly sliced

½ tsp garlic granules or garlic powder

½ tsp ground cumin

½ tsp ground turmeric

½ cup (30 g) panko breadcrumbs

⅓ cup (40 g) all-purpose flour or flour of choice

1 large egg, beaten

Salt, as needed (optional, for kids 12+ months)

Black pepper, as needed

2 tbsp (30 ml) avocado or olive oil

Herby Hummus Dip (page 70) or other baby-friendly dip, for serving

Fruit or vegetable of choice, for serving

Fill a medium saucepan half full with water and bring it to a boil over high heat. Reduce the heat to medium and add the lentils. Cook the lentils for 5 minutes. Drain and rinse the lentils with cold water.

Transfer the lentils to a food processor or blender. Add the carrots, scallions, garlic granules, cumin and turmeric. Process the ingredients on low speed until the mixture comes together. Be careful not to overprocess the mixture; otherwise the fritters won't hold their shape.

Transfer the lentil mixture to a large bowl. Add the breadcrumbs, flour, egg, salt (if using) and black pepper. Mix the ingredients until they are well combined. Form the mixture into eight to ten patties, using about ¼ cup (60 g) of the mixture per patty. Place the patties on a plate and chill them in the refrigerator for 20 minutes to firm up.

Heat a large nonstick frying pan over medium heat and add the oil. Once the oil is hot, add the fritters and cook them for 2 to 3 minutes on each side, or until they are golden brown and crispy. You may need to cook the fritters in batches. Transfer the fritters to a layer of paper towels to drain.

Serve the fritters whole, cut in half or cut into strips with the Herby Hummus Dip and the fruit or vegetable on the side. Some babies may squish a whole fritter in their hands instead of tasting it, so you may find that serving it as strips is easier for them to pick up and bite. For older babies working on their pincer grasp, you can cut fritters into smaller pieces.

Store the fritters in an airtight container in the refrigerator for up to 3 days. To freeze, stack the fritters between sheets of parchment paper in a freezer bag and freeze them for up to 3 months. Thaw the fritters in the refrigerator or at room temperature before reheating in the oven at 400°F (200°C, gas mark 6) for 10 to 15 minutes, or until warmed through.

Prep Time:
10 minutes + 20 minutes to chill

Cook Time:
4 to 6 minutes per batch

Yield:
8 to 10 fritters

MAKE-AHEAD

FREEZER FRIENDLY

LUNCHBOX FRIENDLY

VEGETARIAN

DAIRY FREE

NUT FREE

SOURCE OF IRON, PROTEIN & FIBER

Peanut Butter Banana Bread

I'm not particularly fancy when it comes to using up those overripe bananas that always seem to crowd the fruit bowl, and I'd be quite happy to make traditional banana bread each and every time my bananas get a little too ripe. My family members, however, have different ideas. And after one too many half-eaten banana loaves, I realized it was time to make a change.

Adding peanut butter to banana bread is a simple but effective way to switch up this classic baked treat. It's a strong enough flavor to take the loaf to another level, but it doesn't cover up the banana flavor—which is just as well, because peanut and banana make for a fantastic combination. And, of course, you can't go wrong with that extra boost of iron and protein—it works brilliantly!

Prep Time:
8 minutes

Cook Time:
35 to 45 minutes

Yield:
1 (2-lb [907-g]) loaf

MAKE-AHEAD

FREEZER FRIENDLY

LUNCHBOX FRIENDLY

VEGETARIAN

DAIRY-FREE OPTION

SOURCE OF IRON & PROTEIN

Nonstick cooking spray, as needed

1 cup (125 g) all-purpose flour

½ cup (60 g) whole wheat flour

1 tsp baking powder

1 tsp baking soda

1 tsp ground cinnamon

1 large egg

⅓ cup (85 g) smooth 100% natural peanut butter

¼ tsp salt (optional, for kids 12+ months)

3 medium-size very ripe bananas, mashed

¼ cup (60 ml) full-fat milk or nondairy milk

¼ cup (60 ml) melted butter or coconut oil, slightly cooled

¼ cup (60 ml) pure maple syrup (optional)

Full-fat plain Greek, natural or nondairy yogurt, for serving

Fruit of choice, for serving

Preheat the oven to 375°F (190°C, gas mark 5). Line a 9 x 5-inch (23 x 13-cm) loaf pan with parchment paper and spray it with the nonstick cooking spray.

In a large bowl, mix together the all-purpose flour, whole wheat flour, baking powder, baking soda and cinnamon. In a medium bowl, whisk together the egg, peanut butter, salt (if using), bananas, milk, butter and maple syrup (if using) until the ingredients are well combined.

Add the egg mixture to the flour mixture and, with a wooden spoon, gently mix the two until they are just combined—do not overmix the batter, or the bread will be dense. Pour the batter into the prepared loaf pan and bake the bread for 35 to 45 minutes, or until it is golden brown and a toothpick inserted into the center comes out clean. If after 35 minutes the bread is golden brown but is not yet cooked in the middle, loosely cover it with aluminum foil so it can finish baking without burning.

Allow the bread to cool before removing it from the loaf pan. Cut it into slices around the same thickness of your index or middle finger, then slice those in half lengthwise. The bread will be soft, and your baby may squish it with their hands and break it apart—this is okay and will allow them to practice picking up smaller pieces with their pincer grasp. Serve the bread as part of a snack or for breakfast with the yogurt and fruit, or pack it in a lunchbox for eating on the go.

Store the bread in an airtight container on the countertop for up to 3 days. To freeze the bread, slice the loaf, stack the slices between sheets of parchment paper in a freezer bag and freeze them for up to 3 months. Thaw the bread in the refrigerator or at room temperature. The frozen bread can also be packed in a lunchbox, and it will thaw in 1 to 2 hours.

Sweet Potato and Broccoli Tots

When my son was starting out with baby-led weaning, one of his favorite things to eat was homemade broccoli tots. They were super soft and easy for him to hold, so they worked perfectly as a first food. Roll on to toddlerhood: He still loves them, and over time my recipe has evolved to ramp up the nutrition and flavor and make them more appealing to adults too.

This version is vegetarian, but this recipe works well with cooked flaked fish, especially salmon, so feel free to add any leftover fish you may have on hand. This recipe also works with leftover mashed potatoes. Just be sure to use chilled mashed potatoes—otherwise, the tots will be too soft to hold their shape.

Prep Time:
15 minutes

Cook Time:
18 to 20 minutes

Yield:
12 to 14 tots

1 cup (175 g) fresh or frozen broccoli florets

2 medium sweet potatoes

Nonstick cooking spray, as needed

½ cup (50 g) dried breadcrumbs (see Cook's Tip)

¼ cup (25 g) grated Parmesan cheese

2 tbsp (6 g) finely chopped fresh chives or 2 tsp (2 g) dried chives

½ tsp garlic granules or garlic powder

Black pepper, as needed

Iron source (such as eggs), for serving

Vegetable or fruit of choice, for serving

Bring a small pot of water to boil over high heat. Add the broccoli. If you are using fresh broccoli, cook it for 8 to 10 minutes, or until it is fork-tender. If you are using frozen broccoli, cook it for 6 to 8 minutes, or until it is tender. Alternatively, steam the broccoli for 10 to 12 minutes, or until it is fork-tender. Drain the broccoli and set aside.

Meanwhile, pierce the sweet potatoes several times with a fork and microwave them on high for 6 to 8 minutes, or until the flesh inside is soft. Once the sweet potatoes are cooked, carefully cut them in half. Set the sweet potatoes aside to cool slightly.

Preheat the oven to 400°F (200°C, gas mark 6). Line a medium baking sheet with parchment paper and spray the parchment paper with the nonstick cooking spray.

When the sweet potatoes are cool enough to handle, scoop out the flesh and place it in a large bowl. Add the broccoli, and mash the sweet potatoes and broccoli together with a fork, making sure to break up the broccoli well.

Add the breadcrumbs, Parmesan cheese, chives, garlic granules and black pepper, and mix the ingredients together until everything is well combined. Shape the mixture into tater tot shapes, using 2 tablespoons (30 g) of the mixture for each tot, and arrange the tots on the prepared baking sheet (see Nutritionist's Tip). Bake the tots for 18 to 20 minutes, or until they are golden.

Allow the tots to cool before using a spatula to gently ease them off the baking sheet. Serve the tots as part of a snack or for lunch with an iron source, such as eggs, and a vegetable or fruit on the side.

(Continued)

MAKE-AHEAD

FREEZER FRIENDLY

LUNCHBOX FRIENDLY

VEGETARIAN

EGG FREE

NUT FREE

SOURCE OF FIBER

Sweet Potato and Broccoli Tots (Continued)

Store the tots in an airtight container in the refrigerator for up to 3 days. To freeze the tots, arrange the cooled tots on a baking sheet and flash-freeze them for 1 hour. Transfer the tots to a freezer bag and keep them in the freezer for up to 3 months. To reheat the tots, place the frozen tots on a baking sheet lined with parchment paper, and bake them in the oven at 350°F (180°C, gas mark 4) for 15 to 20 minutes, or until they are heated through.

NUTRITIONIST'S TIP: For early eaters, try shaping these tots into finger shapes too! Different babies will like different things, and a longer shape might mean your baby has more success getting them into their mouth in the beginning.

COOK'S TIP: In a pinch, you can use panko breadcrumbs instead of traditional.

Vanilla Oat Waffles

Eating waffles for breakfast brings back such fond memories of my childhood. Back then it was considered a treat, and one we only had on special occasions with mountains of fruit and lashings of whipped cream. It was my favorite breakfast!

I wanted to create these memories with my own kids, but without limiting waffles to just special occasions. This is where traditional waffles get a nutritious makeover, but one that doesn't compromise on that classic waffle texture and flavor kids love. Swapping out plain white flour for oats gives these waffles a boost of iron, and using vanilla extract is great for adding flavor without using sugar. What's more, if you don't have a waffle maker, you can use this batter to make fluffy oat pancakes instead!

3 cups (270 g) rolled oats

1 tbsp (15 g) baking powder

3 large eggs

1¼ cups (300 ml) full-fat cow's milk (see Cook's Tip)

2 tsp (10 ml) pure vanilla extract

¼ cup (60 ml) melted butter or coconut oil, slightly cooled

Nonstick cooking spray, as needed

Fruit of choice, for serving

Pure maple syrup, for serving (optional)

Full-fat plain Greek or natural yogurt, applesauce or freshly whipped heavy cream, for serving

In a blender, combine the oats, baking powder, eggs, milk, vanilla and butter. Blend the ingredients on high speed for 30 seconds. Remove the blender's lid, scrape down the sides and then blend again until the batter is well-blended—a grainy texture is okay. Allow the batter to rest for 10 minutes—do not skip this step, as it's what makes the waffles crispy and the pancakes fluffy.

FOR WAFFLES

Preheat a waffle maker and spray it with the nonstick cooking spray. Pour in the amount of batter recommended by the waffle maker's manufacturer. Cook the waffles for 3 to 4 minutes, until they are golden and crispy, or follow the manufacturer's instructions for your particular waffle maker. Remove the waffles from the waffle maker, set them aside and repeat this process with the remaining batter.

FOR PANCAKES

Heat a large nonstick frying pan over medium heat. Spray the frying pan with the nonstick cooking spray. Add ¼-cup (60-ml) dollops of the batter to the frying pan. Cook the pancakes for 1 to 2 minutes, until the undersides are golden. Flip the pancakes and cook them for 1 minute, or until the bottoms are golden. Remove the pancakes from the frying pan, set them aside and repeat this process with the remaining batter.

(Continued)

Prep Time:
5 minutes +
10 minutes to rest

Cook Time:
3 to 4 minutes
for waffles; 2 to
3 minutes for
pancakes

Yield:
Serves 3 adults +
3 children

30
30 MINUTES OR
LESS

MAKE-AHEAD

FREEZER
FRIENDLY

LUNCHBOX
FRIENDLY

VEGETARIAN

NUT FREE

SOU

Vanilla Oat Waffles (Continued)

SERVING AND STORAGE

Cut the waffles or pancakes into stick shapes for early eaters, or into bite-sized pieces for babies working on their pincer grasp. Serve them with the fruit, maple syrup (if using) and yogurt (see Nutritionist's Tip).

Store the waffles or pancakes in an airtight container in the refrigerator for up to 3 days. To freeze them, arrange the cooled waffles or pancakes on a large baking sheet and flash-freeze them for 1 hour. Transfer the waffles or pancakes to a freezer bag and keep them in the freezer for up to 3 months.

Reheat frozen waffles in the toaster on the lowest setting until they are warmed through. Reheat frozen pancakes by placing them in an even layer on a large baking sheet. Cover them with aluminum foil and heat them in the oven at 350°F (180°C, gas mark 4) for 10 minutes, until they are warm and soft.

NUTRITIONIST'S TIP: Waffles are a great finger food for babies, but some children can have a hard time with them. If this is your baby, try spreading yogurt on the waffle or soaking it in some warm milk for a few minutes before serving. Both options will make the texture more manageable.

COOK'S TIP: Cow's milk is essential to this recipe. I've tested various milks for this recipe—including nondairy milks—and the results are not consistent.

Salmon and Pea Egg Muffins

I have a special love for these muffins. They brought my son, an infant at the time, around to eating eggs after a lengthy standoff of several months when he refused to eat anything even slightly eggy. Of course, these are not magical muffins, and they may not win over every egg-resistant baby or toddler, but they are a great place to start!

These muffins are perfect for lunchboxes and eating on the go. And they're a great source of protein, iron and healthy fats, so they will leave both kids and adults feeling satisfied. You can also omit the frozen peas and use leftover cooked veggies—broccoli works very well, as do asparagus and zucchini. You could even pop a few cherry or grape tomatoes on top if you fancy it!

Nonstick cooking spray, as needed

6 large or 8 medium eggs

¼ cup (60 ml) full-fat milk or nondairy milk

¼ cup (15 g) finely chopped scallions

½ cup (55 g) grated Cheddar cheese

1 tsp garlic granules or garlic powder

1 tsp dried oregano

Black pepper, as needed

1 (5-oz [145-g]) can skinless, boneless salmon or leftover cooked salmon, flaked

¼ cup (35 g) frozen peas

High-calorie food (such as sweet potato wedges, buttered toast or a whole-grain waffle), for serving

Fruit of choice, for serving (optional)

COOK'S TIP: If you have a mini 24-cup muffin pan, reduce the cooking time by 5 to 7 minutes. Mini muffins are the perfect size for babies to handle, they are great for lunchboxes and they can help reduce food waste when feeding younger babies.

Preheat the oven to 350°F (180°C, gas mark 4). Line a 12-cup muffin pan with silicone cupcake liners. Alternatively, spray the muffin pan liberally with nonstick cooking spray. Avoid baking the muffins in paper liners, as they tend to stick and can be difficult to remove.

Crack the eggs into a large bowl. Add the milk and whisk the eggs and milk together until the mixture is smooth and frothy. Add the scallions, Cheddar cheese, garlic granules, oregano and black pepper, and whisk again to combine the ingredients.

Evenly divide the salmon between the muffin cups. Carefully fill each cup three-fourths full with the egg mixture. Top each muffin with a few frozen peas.

Bake the muffins for 20 to 25 minutes, or until they are golden and the eggs have fully set.

Allow the muffins to cool in the pan for 5 to 10 minutes before removing them from the pan. Cut the muffins in half for early eaters or in quarters for older babies, or you can leave them whole if preferred. Your baby or toddler may enjoy picking the pieces of salmon and peas out of the muffins to eat separately, which will be easier for them to do if the muffins are cut before serving. Serve the muffins alongside the high-calorie food and fruit, if you wish.

Store the muffins in an airtight container in the refrigerator for up to 3 days. To freeze them, place the cooled muffins in a freezer bag in an even layer and freeze them for up to 3 months. Defrost the muffins in the refrigerator or at room temperature before reheating them in the oven at 350°F (180°C, gas mark 4) for 10 to 15 minutes, or until they are warmed through. You can also microwave them on high for 20 to 30 seconds, or until they are warmed through.

Prep Time:
6 minutes

Cook Time:
20 to 25 minutes

Yield:
12 muffins

MAKE-AHEAD

FREEZER FRIENDLY

LUNCHBOX FRIENDLY

NUT FREE

SOURCE OF IRON & PROTEIN

Savory Snack Bars

Rolled oats are among the top BLW foods for both practicality and versatility. They are affordable, easy to find, nutritious and—most importantly—they taste good! Not only that, they are great for texture exploration, as they can be messy, soft, firm, creamy, crumbly and even sticky. I have a few oat-based recipes in this cookbook, and this is my savory offering. Packed with veggies you'll likely have on hand and gently flavored with cheese, scallions and herbs, these snack bars are firm but moist, making them a great option for baby finger foods. They also make for super quick snacks and fuss-free eating on the go.

I often serve these as a quick lunch with a dollop of hummus or a serving of coleslaw and a salad (for the adults) or with some broccoli on the side. They are also great for school lunchboxes, as they are nut free.

Prep Time:
10 minutes

Cook Time:
30 to 35 minutes

Yield:
8 full bars or 16 half bars

MAKE-AHEAD

FREEZER FRIENDLY

LUNCHBOX FRIENDLY

VEGETARIAN

NUT FREE

SOURCE OF IRON & FIBER

Nonstick cooking spray, as needed

1½ cups (135 g) rolled oats (see Cook's Tip)

½ tsp dried sage or thyme

½ cup (55 g) shredded carrots

½ cup (60 g) shredded zucchini

1 finely chopped scallion

⅔ cup (75 g) grated Cheddar cheese

2 large eggs, beaten

¼ cup (60 ml) full-fat milk or milk of choice

2 tbsp (30 ml) melted unsalted butter

Black pepper, as needed

Sliced, cubed or mashed avocado, for serving

Steamed or roasted vegetables of choice, for serving

Preheat the oven to 350°F (180°C, gas mark 4). Line a 9 x 5-inch (23 x 13-cm) loaf pan with parchment paper, and then spray the parchment paper with the nonstick cooking spray.

In a large bowl, combine the oats, sage, carrots, zucchini, scallion, Cheddar cheese, eggs, milk, butter and black pepper, and mix the ingredients together. Transfer the mixture to the prepared loaf pan and use the back of a spoon to spread it out in the pan and smooth the top.

Bake the snack bar mixture for 30 to 35 minutes, or until it is cooked through and golden. Allow it to cool completely before removing it from the loaf pan and slicing it into 8 bars or 16 half bars for younger babies. You can break these bars up into smaller pieces for babies working on their pincer grasp, but you may prefer to skip this if you are packing the bars to eat on the go. Serve the bars as part of a snack or for lunch with the avocado and vegetables on the side. Or pack the bars in a lunchbox for eating on the go.

Store the bars in an airtight container in the refrigerator for up to 3 days. To freeze them, arrange the bars on a large baking sheet and flash-freeze them for 1 hour. Transfer them to a freezer bag and keep them in the freezer for up to 3 months. Defrost the bars in the refrigerator or at room temperature. The frozen bars can also be packed in a lunchbox, and they will thaw in 1 to 2 hours.

COOK'S TIP: Stick with regular rolled oats for this recipe, and avoid using instant or steel-cut oats; otherwise, the texture of the bars will be either too soft or not soft enough!

Tuna and Chickpea Fritters

I've already talked about my love for fritters, and this cookbook wouldn't be complete if I didn't include this recipe, which is a family favorite! A great way to incorporate fish into your baby's diet, these gorgeously golden and crispy fritters are packed full of iron and have a deep earthy flavor that complements the tuna without making it overpowering. This recipe is a great choice for kids who are still learning to like fish. Feel free to switch out the tuna for canned salmon or another cooked flaky fish. You can also switch out the broccoli for other veggies, such as grated carrot or zucchini, and play around with the spices to suit your personal tastes.

1 (15-oz [400-g]) can chickpeas, drained and rinsed

1 (5-oz [145-g]) can tuna, drained

1 cup (90 g) finely chopped or grated broccoli florets

1 to 2 large eggs, beaten

¼ cup (15 g) finely chopped scallions

¼ cup (30 g) all-purpose flour

1 tsp garlic granules or garlic powder

1 tsp Old Bay Seasoning or smoked paprika, or to taste

Salt, as needed (optional, for kids 12+ months)

Black pepper, as needed

2 tbsp (30 ml) avocado or other high-heat oil

Fruit or vegetable of choice, for serving

Cottage cheese, for serving (optional)

In a large bowl, mash the chickpeas with a fork. You can also use a blender for this, but make sure there is still some texture left to the chickpeas—you don't want a smooth paste.

Add the tuna, broccoli, 1 egg, scallions, flour, garlic granules, Old Bay Seasoning, salt (if using) and black pepper to the chickpeas and use a fork to mix everything together until the ingredients are well combined. If it seems too crumbly to shape, add a second beaten egg. Shape the mixture into ¼-cup (60-g) patties and chill them in the refrigerator for 20 minutes to firm up.

Heat a large nonstick frying pan over medium heat and add the oil. Once the oil is hot, add the fritters and cook them for 3 to 4 minutes on each side, or until they are golden brown and crispy. Drain the fritters on paper towels and allow them to cool before serving.

Leave the fritters whole or cut them in half or into strips. Some babies may squish a whole fritter in their hands instead of tasting it, so you may find that serving it in strips is easier for your child to pick up and bite. For older babies working on their pincer grasp, you can cut the fritters into smaller pieces. Serve the fritters as part of a snack or for lunch alongside the fruit or vegetable and a small dollop of cottage cheese (if using).

Store the fritters in an airtight container in the refrigerator for up to 3 days. To freeze the fritters, stack them between sheets of parchment paper in a freezer bag and freeze them for up to 3 months. Thaw the fritters before reheating them in the oven at 400°F (200°C, gas mark 6) for 10 to 15 minutes, or until heated through.

NUTRITIONIST'S TIP: Tuna is a great option for babies right from the start of eating. Aim for chunk light (skipjack) tuna, though, as albacore can be much higher in mercury.

Prep Time:
10 minutes +
20 minutes to
chill

Cook Time:
6 to 8 minutes

Yield:
10 to 12 fritters

MAKE-AHEAD

FREEZER FRIENDLY

LUNCHBOX FRIENDLY

DAIRY-FREE OPTION

NUT FREE

SOURCE OF IRON, PROTEIN & FIBER

Prep Time:
7 minutes

Cook Time:
20 to 22 minutes

Yield:
10 muffins

30 MINUTES OR LESS

MAKE-AHEAD

FREEZER FRIENDLY

LUNCHBOX FRIENDLY

VEGETARIAN

DAIRY-FREE OPTION

NUT FREE

Mixed Berry Muffins

Perfect for little hands, these soft and fluffy muffins are moist, satisfying and gently flavored with the tartness of the berries and a hint of sweet cinnamon. For younger babies and toddlers, the berries do a great job of sweetening the muffins naturally, but for older kids and adults, you may prefer to use maple syrup to give them that extra oomph. Just be sure to use 100 percent pure maple syrup, as it is free from additives and the true-to-nature flavor is well worth it!

1 cup (125 g) all-purpose flour

½ cup (60 g) whole wheat flour

2 tsp (10 g) baking powder

½ tsp ground cinnamon

¼ tsp salt (optional, for kids 12+ months)

2 large eggs

¼ cup (60 ml) melted and cooled coconut oil or extra virgin olive oil

⅓ cup (80 ml) full-fat milk or nondairy milk, plus more as needed

¼ cup (60 ml) pure maple syrup (optional)

1 tsp pure vanilla extract

½ cup (60 g) frozen or fresh blueberries

½ cup (60 g) frozen or fresh raspberries, roughly chopped

Full-fat plain Greek or natural yogurt or scrambled eggs, for serving

Preheat the oven to 400°F (200°C, gas mark 6). Line a 12-cup muffin pan with 10 cupcake liners.

In a large bowl, mix together the all-purpose flour, whole wheat flour, baking powder, cinnamon and salt (if using). In a medium bowl, combine the eggs, oil, milk, maple syrup (if using) and vanilla. Whisk the ingredients together until they are smooth.

Add the egg mixture to the flour mixture. Using a wooden spoon, gently mix them together until they are just combined—do not overmix or the muffins will be dense. The batter will be thick and will have some lumps, which is fine. If your batter is too thick to scoop, add a little more milk. Gently fold the blueberries and raspberries into the batter until they are just combined.

Divide the batter evenly among the 10 muffin liners. Bake the muffins for 20 to 22 minutes, or until they are golden and a toothpick inserted into the center of a muffin comes out clean of wet batter. If you did not include the maple syrup, check them at the 18-minute mark, as they may cook quicker.

Cut the muffins in half for early eaters or in quarters for older babies. You may also leave them whole if preferred. If your baby likes to take huge bites of food, you may find it easier to cut the muffins into quarters and serve one or two pieces at a time. Serve the muffins as a snack with a dollop of yogurt or as part of a balanced breakfast with some scrambled eggs.

Store the muffins on the countertop in an airtight container for up to 3 days. To freeze the muffins, place the cooled muffins in a freezer bag in an even layer and freeze them for up to 3 months. Thaw them in the refrigerator or at room temperature. The frozen muffins can also be packed in a lunchbox, and they will thaw in 1 to 2 hours.

COOK'S TIP: You can use any berries you like for this recipe, just be sure to cut them similar in size and no bigger than a blueberry, so that the muffins will cook evenly.

Crispy Coconut Chicken Tenders

Crispy, juicy coconutty chicken tenders: These are what I like to think of as fancy chicken nuggets! They are the perfect shape for babies just starting on solids, and the slightly sweet coconut notes give a welcome twist to this family favorite.

Another plus is that these chicken tenders can be cooked straight from the freezer, so you get the same convenience of a store-bought version, but with a more grown-up flavor and texture that appeals to both adults and little ones. In the unlikely event that you have leftovers, they make for a truly mouthwatering chicken burger for lunch the next day!

2 large eggs

2 tsp (10 g) Dijon mustard

¼ cup (30 g) all-purpose flour

1 tsp garlic granules or garlic powder

1 tsp onion granules or onion powder

1 tsp dried basil

Salt, as needed (optional, for kids 12+ months)

Black pepper, as needed

1 lb (450 g) boneless, skinless chicken breasts

1 cup (60 g) panko breadcrumbs

½ cup (50 g) unsweetened shredded coconut

¼ cup (60 ml) avocado or high-heat oil of choice for the stove method

Carbohydrate of choice or low-sodium, low-sugar canned baked beans, for serving

Vegetables of choice, for serving

Crack the eggs into a medium bowl. Add the mustard and whisk until smooth. Add the flour, garlic granules, onion granules, basil, salt (if using) and black pepper. Whisk the ingredients again until a smooth batter forms. Cut the chicken breasts into strips about the width and length of one to two adult fingers. Add the chicken to the bowl and stir until all of the strips are coated in the batter. Set the bowl aside.

In a shallow baking dish or bowl, mix together the breadcrumbs and coconut. Roll one piece of chicken at a time in the breadcrumb mixture and transfer the chicken to a dry plate.

STOVE

Heat a large nonstick frying pan over medium-high heat and add the oil. Once the oil is hot, add the chicken strips in an even layer, being sure not to overcrowd the frying pan. Fry the chicken for 5 to 6 minutes on both sides, or until the tenders are crispy and golden and the chicken is fully cooked through. Transfer the chicken tenders to a layer of paper towels to drain.

OVEN

Preheat the oven to 400°F (200°C, gas mark 6). Line a large baking sheet with parchment paper. Place the chicken tenders on the prepared baking sheet. Bake the chicken tenders for 25 to 30 minutes, or until they are golden and fully cooked through.

(Continued)

Prep Time:
10 minutes

Cook Time:
10 to 12 minutes on the stove; 25 to 30 minutes in the oven

Yield:
Serves 2 adults + 2 children

30 MINUTES OR LESS

MAKE-AHEAD

FREEZER FRIENDLY

DAIRY-FREE

NUT FREE

SOURCE OF IRON & PROTEIN

Crispy Coconut Chicken Tenders (Continued)

SERVING AND STORAGE

These tenders are the perfect shape for younger babies to hold, but you may find that they mostly suck off the breading or gnaw on the chicken. This is totally normal for early eaters and is a part of the learning process. Babies will soon learn how to bite off pieces of chicken with their gums or teeth. As your baby further develops their pincer grasp, you can cut the chicken tenders into bite-sized pieces. Serve the chicken tenders with the carbohydrate of choice and a side of vegetables.

Store the chicken tenders in an airtight container in the refrigerator for up to 3 days. To freeze the chicken tenders, arrange the cooled tenders on a large baking sheet and flash-freeze them for 1 hour. Transfer the tenders to a freezer bag and keep them in the freezer for up to 3 months. To reheat the frozen chicken tenders, place them on a large baking sheet lined with parchment paper and bake them at 350°F (180°C, gas mark 4) for 30 to 35 minutes, or until they are heated through.

COOK'S TIP: Switch things up by using the coconutty breadcrumb mixture to make fish sticks!

Sausage and Herb Pinwheels

Pinwheels are a baby-led weaning classic that have proven to be very popular in recent years. Their flat, circular shape makes them easy for little hands to hold, and they can be popped into lunchboxes for fuss-free eating on the go. What I love most about them is how versatile they are; they can be sweet, savory, light or hearty and can take on virtually any flavor you desire.

For this recipe, I have used sausage and herbs, which makes this an easy and safe way to serve pork to your baby. This particular pinwheel recipe is also a great source of iron. Other variations you may wish to try are chopped baby spinach and Cheddar cheese; Chia Jam (page 69), blueberries and cinnamon; Tomato Sauce (page 81) and mozzarella cheese; or even leftover Shredded Beef Brisket (page 137), taco meat or spaghetti sauce!

Nonstick cooking spray, as needed

1 tsp dried chives

1 tsp dried parsley

½ tsp dried thyme

1 large egg

1 tbsp (10 g) flour of choice

1 (14 x 9" [35 x 23–cm]) sheet thawed rolled puff pastry (see Cook's Tip)

1 tbsp (15 g) Dijon mustard

1 lb (450 g) ground pork sausage

Black pepper, as needed

Fruit of choice or steamed or roasted broccoli, for serving

Preheat the oven to 400°F (200°C, gas mark 6). Line a large baking sheet with parchment paper and spray the paper with the nonstick cooking spray.

In a small bowl, mix together the chives, parsley and thyme. In another small bowl, whisk the egg. Set the bowls aside.

Dust a work surface with the flour and gently unroll the puff pastry, so that the longest side is facing you. Using a spatula, thinly spread the mustard onto the pastry, leaving a roughly ¾-inch (2-cm) border around the edges.

Place the sausage in a large bowl. Knead the meat with your hands until it is soft and pliable. Spread it evenly onto the puff pastry, pushing it into place with your fingers, while still maintaining the border around the edges. Sprinkle the sausage with the herb mixture and the black pepper.

Starting with the side closest to you, gently roll the pastry away from you to create a log shape. Stop rolling once you reach the border and use a pastry brush to brush the beaten egg along the border, reserving some for later. Finish rolling the pastry and press the border down to seal the edges.

Using a sharp serrated knife, slice the log into eight equal pieces. Lay each piece, meat side facing up and down, on the prepared baking sheet. Gently press the pinwheels down with a solid spatula. Brush each pinwheel generously with the beaten egg. Bake the pinwheels for 25 to 30 minutes, or until they are golden and the sausage is cooked through (internal temperature of 160°F [71°C]). Allow the pinwheels to cool slightly before serving.

(Continued)

Prep Time:
10 minutes

Cook Time:
25 to 30 minutes

Yield:
8 pinwheels

MAKE-AHEAD

FREEZER FRIENDLY

LUNCHBOX FRIENDLY

NUT FREE

SOURCE OF IRON & PROTEIN

Sausage and Herb Pinwheels (Continued)

These pinwheels are best served whole or cut in half for babies and toddlers of all ages, so that they can hold their shape while being eaten. Your baby might just suck on the pastry, but little bits will break off and melt in their mouth to make it easier for them to get to the sausage. Try serving the pinwheels as a snack with some fruit or alongside some steamed or roasted broccoli for dinner.

Store the pinwheels in an airtight container in the refrigerator for up to 3 days. To freeze the pinwheels, stack them between sheets of parchment paper in a freezer bag and freeze them for up to 3 months. To reheat frozen pinwheels, place them on a large baking sheet and bake them in the oven at 350°F (180°C, gas mark 4) for 20 to 25 minutes, or until they are heated through.

COOK'S TIP: If you are in the United Kingdom, note that the puff pastry listed in this recipe is equal to 1 (11-oz [312-g]) packet of frozen puff pastry.

NUTRITIONIST'S TIP: A pinwheel is a great way to expose your baby to lots of different flavors in one small package. Adding a meat to the pinwheel gives you a balanced option that serves as a good source of iron.

Tropical Frozen Yogurt Bark

Frozen yogurt bark ticks many boxes when it comes to feeding babies and toddlers. Not only is it a convenient breakfast and snack option, but it also makes for a deliciously creamy, satisfying and nutritious dessert. Another plus is that it works wonders to soothe sore teething gums and helps keep babies and toddlers cool on hot summer days.

My kids have tried many combinations of yogurt bark, and they all agree that they prefer the refreshing taste of the tropics, which reminds them of our family vacation in Jamaica. If you are having difficulty finding these ingredients or they are out of season, you can substitute any or all of the toppings with other fruits of your choice.

17 oz (500 g) plain full-fat Greek yogurt

2 tbsp (30 ml) pure maple syrup (optional; see Cook's Tips)

1 to 2 medium passion fruits (see Cook's Tips)

1 medium mango, peeled and diced

1 medium kiwi, peeled and diced

1 tbsp (6 g) unsweetened shredded coconut

1 tbsp (10 g) hemp seeds

Line a medium baking sheet with parchment paper, making sure to leave some excess paper around the sides of the baking sheet so that you can easily lift out the yogurt bark once it is frozen. Set the baking sheet aside.

In a medium bowl, mix together the yogurt and maple syrup (if using) until they are well combined. Pour the mixture onto the prepared baking sheet. Use a spatula to spread the yogurt mixture out to an even thickness of approximately ½ inch (1 cm).

Cut open 1 passion fruit. Scoop out the flesh and spoon it over the yogurt as evenly as you can. Some passion fruits are fleshier than others, so you may find that you won't need to use the other passion fruit. Arrange the mango and kiwi over the yogurt. Sprinkle the yogurt with the coconut and hemp seeds.

Place the baking sheet into the freezer, making sure it is sitting completely level. Freeze the yogurt bark for 4 hours, or until it is frozen solid. Remove the baking sheet from the freezer and break up the yogurt bark into easy-to-hold pieces. Transfer the pieces to a freezer bag and keep them in the freezer for up to 3 months. Your baby will likely suck and gnaw on pieces of yogurt bark instead of taking bites, which can often be quite messy but will be great for sensory exploration.

COOK'S TIPS: Instead of maple syrup, use pureed fruit pouches to naturally sweeten the yogurt and add another layer of flavor.

If you can't find fresh passion fruits, try looking in the freezer section of the grocery store for frozen pureed passion fruit. Defrost before using in the recipe.

Prep Time:
8 minutes

Freeze Time:
4 hours

Yield:
Approximately 19 oz (539 g)

MAKE-AHEAD

FREEZER FRIENDLY

VEGETARIAN

EGG FREE

NUT FREE

SOURCE OF PROTEIN

MESSY MEAL

Prep Time:
8 minutes

Cook Time:
12 to 14 minutes

Yield:
16 sticks

30 MINUTES OR LESS

MAKE-AHEAD

FREEZER FRIENDLY

DAIRY-FREE OPTION

NUT FREE

SOURCE OF IRON

Spinach and Banana French Toast Sticks

French toast is one of those foods that makes me think of lazy Saturday mornings, when you get to sleep late and take your time making breakfast for the family. But let's be real—with a baby or toddler on deck, your Saturday mornings probably don't look like that anymore! That doesn't mean you can't whip up some comforting, nutritious French toast thanks to having previously baked and frozen a batch. Besides the fact that these beauties can be reheated straight from the freezer, what I love most is that they are naturally sweetened with banana and get a boost of iron from the spinach. We call them "Hulk toasts," and my kids absolutely love them! Even better, you don't have to stand at the stove flipping them, as the oven does all the work for you.

Nonstick cooking spray, as needed

1½ cups (45 g) tightly packed fresh baby spinach

2 small bananas

2 large eggs

½ cup (120 ml) full-fat milk or nondairy milk

1 tsp pure vanilla extract

4 thick slices whole wheat or white bread

Full-fat plain Greek or natural yogurt, for serving (optional)

Fruit of choice, for serving

Pure maple syrup, for serving (optional)

GOOD TO KNOW:
The soaked French toast sticks can also be pan-fried in butter the traditional way. If you choose to cook them this way, use day-old or slightly stale bread instead of fresh. Cook them in a large skillet over medium-high heat for 2 to 3 minutes per side.

Preheat the oven to 375°F (190°C, gas mark 5). Line a large baking sheet with parchment paper and spray the paper with the nonstick cooking spray.

In a blender or food processor, combine the spinach, bananas, eggs, milk and vanilla. Blend the ingredients on high speed until a smooth batter forms. Pour the batter into a wide, shallow baking dish. Set the dish aside.

Cut each slice of bread widthwise into four even pieces. Stir the batter, then place each piece of bread into the batter to soak for 15 seconds on each side. Carefully transfer the bread to the prepared baking sheet, making sure to arrange the bread pieces in an even layer. Bake the French toast sticks for 12 to 14 minutes, or until they are slightly browned and crispy on the edges. Allow them to cool for about 2 minutes before using a spatula to gently loosen them from the baking sheet.

These French toast sticks are the perfect shape for younger babies to hold and bring to their mouths, but you may wish to cut them into smaller pieces for older babies. Bear in mind some older babies and toddlers will enjoy dipping French toast sticks, in which case they may prefer them as sticks. Serve the French toast sticks with the yogurt (if using) and the fruit. For older kids and adults who prefer extra sweetness, drizzle the French toast sticks with the maple syrup (if using).

Store the French toast sticks in an airtight container in the refrigerator for up to 2 days. To freeze, arrange the cooled sticks on a large baking sheet and flash-freeze them for 2 hours. Transfer to a freezer bag and freeze for up to 3 months. Reheat frozen French toast sticks in the oven at 350°F (180°C, gas mark 4) for 8 to 10 minutes, until warmed through. Alternatively, reheat them in the toaster on the low setting until they are warmed through and slightly crisp.

Cheese and Tomato Muffins

Savory muffins gently flavored with Cheddar cheese, oregano and the sweet tang of tomatoes— these delicious muffins are a fantastic finger food for babies, and they are a nutritious on-the-go snack. My toddler loves to eat these warm, cut in half and buttered, but they taste just as good eaten cold too.

I find that when I bake muffins containing cheese, they often stick to paper muffin liners, so avoid paper at all costs! The trick to baking these muffins is to place them directly in a generously greased muffin pan or in silicone or parchment paper muffin liners.

Nonstick cooking spray, as needed

2 large eggs

⅔ cup (160 ml) full-fat cow's milk

3 tbsp (45 g) tomato paste

2 tbsp (30 ml) melted unsalted butter, slightly cooled

½ tsp garlic granules or garlic powder

1 tsp dried oregano

1½ cups (170 g) grated Cheddar cheese

2 cups (250 g) all-purpose flour

2 tsp (10 g) baking powder

12 cherry or grape tomatoes, halved lengthwise

Unsalted butter, for serving

COOK'S TIP:

For additional veggie exposure, add some grated carrot to the batter before baking. Just be sure to squeeze the excess moisture from the grated carrots first, so that the muffins won't be too wet inside!

Preheat the oven to 400°F (200°C, gas mark 6). Generously spray a 12-cup muffin pan with the nonstick cooking spray, or line the cups with silicone or parchment paper muffin liners.

In a large bowl, combine the eggs, milk, tomato paste, butter, garlic granules and oregano. Whisk the ingredients until they are smooth. Add the Cheddar cheese and whisk the mixture again.

Add the flour and baking powder to the egg mixture, and gently mix until just combined—do not overmix the batter, or the muffins will be dense.

Divide the batter evenly among the muffin liners, and place two cherry tomato halves on the top of each muffin, pressing them down a little so they are slightly nestled into the batter. Bake the muffins for 20 to 22 minutes, or until they are golden and a toothpick inserted into the center of a muffin comes out clean of wet batter. Allow the muffins to cool completely before removing them from the muffin pan or liners. If your muffins are sticking to the muffin pan, gently run a knife around the edges to ease them out.

Cut the muffins in half for early eaters or in quarters for older babies. Serve with a little butter spread on top as part of a snack or as an addition to breakfast or lunch. You can also pack them in a lunchbox whole for eating on the go. These are great served at room temperature, but if you want to serve them warm, microwave them for 20 to 30 seconds before serving.

Store the muffins on the countertop in an airtight container for up to 3 days. To freeze the muffins, place cooled muffins in a freezer bag in an even layer and freeze them for up to 3 months. Thaw them in the refrigerator or at room temperature. Frozen muffins can be packed in a lunchbox and will thaw in 1 to 2 hours.

Prep Time:
10 minutes

Cook Time:
20 to 22 minutes

Yield:
12 muffins

MAKE-AHEAD

FREEZER FRIENDLY

LUNCHBOX FRIENDLY

VEGETARIAN

NUT FREE

Green Smoothie Popsicles

Smoothie popsicles are a teething-friendly food and a great opportunity to pack in some extra fruits and veggies. Perfect for all ages, these are zesty, sweet and refreshing, while at the same time being creamy and satisfying.

In addition to their great flavor, these popsicles are a nutrition bomb: They're loaded with iron, healthy fats, fiber, vitamin C and folate! These are perfect for those hot summer days when your baby or toddler isn't eating much and you want to make sure they get a vitamin and mineral boost.

Prep Time:
5 minutes

Freeze Time:
4 hours

Yield:
2 cups (480 ml) liquid smoothie

MAKE–AHEAD

FREEZER FRIENDLY

VEGAN

DAIRY–FREE

EGG FREE

NUT FREE

SOURCE OF IRON

1 cup (30 g) fresh baby spinach

1 medium banana

½ medium avocado

1 cup (165 g) diced fresh or frozen mango

1 medium kiwi, peeled and quartered

1 cup (240 ml) coconut milk or milk of choice (see Cook's Tips)

1 tbsp (10 g) chia seeds

In a blender, combine the spinach, banana, avocado, mango, kiwi, milk and chia seeds. Blend the ingredients on high speed for 1 to 2 minutes, or until the spinach leaves are completely blended.

Distribute the smoothie evenly among the popsicle molds, carefully place the molds in the freezer and freeze the popsicles for at least 4 hours or until frozen solid. When you are ready to serve the popsicles, run a popsicle under warm water to help to loosen it from the mold.

The popsicles will last 3 months in the freezer. Any leftover smoothie can be kept in the refrigerator for up to 24 hours—be sure to give it a stir before serving.

COOK'S TIPS: Double the ingredients so that you can have some smoothie for the adults to drink too. It makes for a super convenient and filling on-the-go breakfast, which will keep you going until lunchtime!

I use coconut milk beverage from a carton, but canned coconut milk or any milk of your choice will work.

Savory Veggie Pancakes

If you're not familiar with savory pancakes, you may be feeling skeptical about this recipe, but let me assure you that these nutritious, veggie-packed delights are not to be dismissed! Not only are they tasty thanks to the warming turmeric and the delicate garlicy notes from the chives, but they are also beautifully crisp on the outside and fluffy and light on the inside.

They're also incredibly convenient, as they can be cooked in the toaster from frozen, making them a great option for a super-quick snack or meal that's also healthy. If your baby or toddler loves pancakes, then be sure to keep things varied by offering them this veggie-packed version.

2 large eggs

½ cup (120 ml) full-fat milk or nondairy milk

⅓ cup (35 g) grated Cheddar cheese

2 tbsp (6 g) finely chopped fresh chives or 2 tsp (2 g) dried chives

⅓ cup (40 g) grated carrots

⅓ cup (55 g) frozen corn (optional; see Cook's Tips)

1 large tomato, seeds removed and diced

1 cup (125 g) all-purpose flour (see Cook's Tips)

1 tsp baking powder

½ tsp garlic granules or garlic powder

¼ tsp ground turmeric

Black pepper, as needed

¼ tsp salt (optional, for kids 12+ months)

1 tbsp (15 ml) avocado or other high-heat oil

Fried egg, for serving

Fruit or vegetable of choice, for serving

In a large bowl, whisk together the eggs and milk until they are smooth. Add the Cheddar cheese, chives, carrots, corn (if using) and tomato and mix to combine.

In a medium bowl, mix together the flour, baking powder, garlic granules, turmeric, black pepper and salt (if using). Add the flour mixture to the egg mixture and use a wooden spoon to mix until well combined.

Heat a large nonstick frying pan over medium heat and add the oil. Once the oil is hot, add 2-tablespoon (30-ml) dollops of the batter to the frying pan. Cook the pancakes for 3 to 4 minutes, or until the undersides are golden. Flip the pancakes and cook them for 2 to 3 minutes, until both sides are golden and crispy. Transfer the pancakes to a layer of paper towels to drain.

For early eaters, cut the pancakes into strips approximately the width of one to two adult fingers. Or cut them into bite-sized pieces for babies who are working on their pincer grasp. Serve the pancakes as a snack or for breakfast or lunch with a fried egg and a serving of fruit or vegetables.

Store in an airtight container in the refrigerator for up to 3 days. To freeze, stack pancakes between sheets of parchment paper in a freezer bag and freeze for up to 3 months. Reheat from frozen in the oven at 350°F (180°C, gas mark 4) for 10 to 15 minutes (covered if you want a softer pancake), or pop into the toaster on the low setting until warmed through and slightly crisp.

COOK'S TIPS: If your baby is younger than 12 months, either mash the corn to make it easier to eat or omit it entirely.

Feel free to use a different type of flour—just add it ¼ cup (30 g) at a time to ensure it doesn't make the batter too thick!

Prep Time:
8 minutes

Cook Time:
5 to 7 minutes per batch

Yield:
10 to 12 pancakes

30 MINUTES OR LESS

MAKE-AHEAD

FREEZER FRIENDLY

LUNCHBOX FRIENDLY

VEGETARIAN

NU

Lemon and Raspberry Oat Cups

Oatmeal gets a busy-morning makeover with these zingy, lemony baked oatmeal cups. Traditionally prepared oatmeal is great for texture exploration and spoon practice, but we don't always have the time to clean up the mammoth mess that is left behind. Baking oatmeal cups ahead of time allows us to offer all the benefits of oatmeal without the mess. Lemon and raspberry are a match made in heaven and work together perfectly in this recipe!

1 cup (90 g) rolled oats

1 tsp baking powder

½ tsp ground cinnamon

⅓ cup (90 g) full-fat plain Greek, natural or nondairy yogurt, plus more for serving (optional)

¼ cup (60 ml) full-fat cow's milk or nondairy milk

1 large egg, beaten

½ tsp pure vanilla extract

2 tbsp (30 ml) pure maple syrup (optional)

Zest of 1 large lemon

8 fresh raspberries

Fruit of choice, for serving

Preheat the oven to 350°F (180°C, gas mark 4). Line a 12-cup muffin pan with 8 muffin liners.

In a large bowl, mix together the oats, baking powder and cinnamon.

In a medium bowl, combine the yogurt, milk, egg, vanilla and maple syrup (if using). Whisk the ingredients until they are smooth.

Add the yogurt mixture to the oat mixture. Use a wooden spoon to mix them until they are well combined. Gently fold in the lemon zest. Divide the mixture evenly between the muffin liners and place 1 raspberry on the top of each oat cup.

Bake the oat cups for 20 to 24 minutes, or until they are golden brown and a toothpick inserted into the center of an oat cup comes out clean of wet batter. Allow the oat cups to cool completely before removing them from the muffin pan and serving.

Cut the oat cups in half for early eaters or into quarters for older babies, or leave them whole if preferred. If your baby likes to take huge bites of food, you may find it easier to quarter the oat cups and serve one or two pieces at a time. Serve the oat cups as a snack or for breakfast with fruit on the side and a dollop of additional yogurt (if using).

Store the oat cups in an airtight container in the refrigerator for up to 3 days. To freeze the oat cups, place the cooled oat cups in a freezer bag in an even layer and freeze them for up to 3 months. Thaw the oat cups in the refrigerator or at room temperature. Frozen oat cups can be packed in a lunchbox, and they will thaw in 1 to 2 hours.

COOK'S TIP: Feel free to play around with the flavors of the oat cups to keep things interesting. Try using orange zest instead of lemon or switching out the yogurt for mashed banana or applesauce, as well as adding different fruits!

Coconut Chia Pudding

Chia seeds! They are all the rage right now, but they mustn't be overlooked as some type of trendy health food that will be long forgotten in a couple of years. Chia seeds are nutritional powerhouses packed full of iron, zinc, calcium, omega-3 and fiber—a great option for your baby or toddler!

My Coconut Chia Pudding is a huge favorite with my kids, and it's a low-effort breakfast that can be made ahead of time. Thanks to the coconut, every spoonful has a distinct nutty and slightly sweet flavor and a wonderfully silky texture. What's more, with a hearty dose of healthy fats from the coconut milk and yogurt, this pudding will leave both kids and adults feeling satisfied until the next meal or snack.

1 cup (240 ml) canned full-fat coconut milk

½ cup (120 ml) full-fat milk or nondairy milk

½ cup (140 g) full-fat plain Greek, natural or nondairy yogurt, plus more as needed

Pure maple syrup, as needed (optional)

¼ cup (40 g) chia seeds

2 tbsp (10 g) unsweetened shredded coconut

Toast, for serving (for babies younger than 12 months)

Fruit of choice, for serving

In a medium bowl, combine the coconut milk, cow's milk, yogurt and maple syrup (if using), and whisk the ingredients together. Add the chia seeds, whisk the mixture again and chill it in the refrigerator for 30 minutes.

After 30 minutes, stir the mixture with a fork to ensure that the chia seeds are evenly distributed. Do not skip this step; otherwise, the chia seeds will clump together. Cover the chia pudding and refrigerate it for at least 8 hours or overnight.

When you're ready to serve, stir the coconut into the pudding. If the pudding has become too thick, thin it with some additional milk before serving. For babies younger than 12 months, spread the pudding thinly onto strips of toast and serve them with a side of fruit. For toddlers, serve the chia pudding in a bowl topped with the fruit.

Alternatively, freeze the chia pudding in popsicle molds prior to serving.

Avoid serving very thick chia pudding on a spoon or in a bowl, as it may glob up, making it hard to swallow. Instead, opt for a runnier consistency when serving chia pudding this way.

As chia seeds are high in fiber, I recommend that a single serving be no more than 2 tablespoons (30 g) for babies 6 to 12 months old and ⅓ cup (80 g) for kids older than 1 year. Chia seeds are great for texture exploration but will be very messy, so you may want to plan ahead for this.

Store the chia pudding in an airtight container in the refrigerator for up to 3 days, or until the milk or yogurt's expiration (whichever is earlier). Frozen popsicles can be stored for up to 3 months.

NUTRITIONIST'S TIP:
Chia seeds are amazingly nutritious! They're full of beneficial nutrients, including fiber and iron. Due to those high nutrient amounts, though, I recommend relatively small serving sizes of chia seeds in the first few months of solid foods.

Prep Time:
3 minutes + 30 minutes to chill

Chill Time:
8 hours or overnight

Yield:
2 cups (480 g)

MAKE-AHEAD

FREEZER FRIENDLY

VEGAN OPTION

DAIRY-FREE OPTION

EGG FREE

NUT FREE

SOURCE OF IRON, PROTEIN & FIBER

MESSY MEAL

Veggie-Loaded Quiche

Quiche is a comforting savory tart that can be served warm or cold, making it perfect for either a comforting dinner or a picnic in the park. One of the reasons I love quiches is that they are great for loading up on veggies and using up whatever you have on hand, including leftover cooked meats and even fish. This recipe takes on a classic feel by using sautéed veggies and is infused with the warming nutty flavors of Parmesan.

Ingredients

1 (9" [23-cm]) unbaked pie crust or 1 sheet (320 g) prepared rolled short-crust pastry

1 tbsp (15 ml) avocado or olive oil

½ cup (40 g) thickly sliced portobello or chestnut mushrooms

½ medium red onion, diced

1 tsp minced garlic

½ small zucchini, sliced into half-moons

6 large eggs

½ cup (120 ml) heavy cream

½ cup (50 g) grated Parmesan cheese

⅓ cup (45 g) frozen peas

Black pepper, as needed

½ cup (75 g) cherry or grape tomatoes, halved lengthwise

Vegetable or fruit of choice, for serving

Instructions

Preheat the oven to 400°F (200°C, gas mark 6). If needed, gently unroll the short-crust pastry and place it into a 9-inch (23-cm) pie dish. Carefully press the pastry into the dish and trim off any excess. Pierce the bottom of the crust several times with a fork. Bake the crust on the middle oven rack for 12 minutes.

Meanwhile, heat a medium frying pan over medium heat and add the oil. Once the oil is hot, add the mushrooms and cook them for 2 to 3 minutes, until they start to brown. Add the onion, garlic and zucchini and stir to combine the vegetables. Cook the mixture for 2 minutes, stirring often, then turn off the heat and set the frying pan aside.

In a large bowl, combine the eggs and heavy cream, and whisk until they are smooth. Add the Parmesan cheese, sautéed vegetables, peas and black pepper. Whisk the mixture until the ingredients are well combined.

Remove the pie dish from the oven and reduce the oven's temperature to 375°F (190°C, gas mark 5). Carefully pour the egg mixture into the pie crust, being careful that it doesn't overflow. Arrange the cherry tomatoes on top of the egg mixture. Bake the quiche for 30 to 35 minutes, or until the filling is fully set.

Allow the quiche to rest until it is cool enough to handle, then cut it into slices for younger babies or into bite-sized pieces for older babies. Your baby may enjoy picking out the individual vegetables, which is a great opportunity for them to explore different textures and tastes. Serve the quiche with an extra vegetable or some fruit on the side.

Store the quiche in an airtight container in the refrigerator for up to 3 days. To freeze the quiche, cover the cooled quiche with aluminum foil, or cut the quiche into slices and stack them between sheets of parchment paper in a freezer bag. Freeze the quiche for up to 3 months. Thaw it in the refrigerator before reheating it in the oven at 350°F (180°C, gas mark 4) for 20 to 25 minutes.

Prep Time:
15 minutes

Cook Time:
30 to 35 minutes

Yield:
1 (9-inch [23-cm]) quiche

MAKE-AHEAD

FREEZER FRIENDLY

LUNCHBOX FRIENDLY

VEGETARIAN

NUT FREE

SOURCE OF IRON & PROTEIN

Peanut Butter and Jam Overnight Oats

Overnight oats are a simple, speedy, nutritious, no-cook breakfast that you can prepare the night before to save yourself time on those crazy-busy mornings. I love to jazz ours up with the classic kid-friendly flavors of peanut butter and jelly. I like to replace traditional jelly with a sugar-free jam made with chia seeds and raspberries, which does a brilliant job of ramping up the nutrition and giving our family a great start to the day!

If you're feeling apprehensive about eating cold oatmeal, you can by all means heat it up before serving, but just be sure to give the cold oats a try first—you will be surprised to learn that they are beautifully soft and delicious, and their consistency is not hard or strange at all. They also make for a great alternative to traditional warm oats during the warmer months of the year.

OVERNIGHT OATS

3 cups (720 ml) full-fat milk or nondairy milk

½ cup (130 g) smooth natural peanut butter

Pure maple syrup or unsweetened applesauce, as needed (optional)

3 cups (270 g) rolled oats

Finely chopped nuts, seeds or shredded coconut, for serving (optional)

2 to 3 medium bananas, thinly sliced or diced, for serving

CHIA JAM

1 cup (150 g) fresh or thawed frozen raspberries

1½ tbsp (15 g) chia seeds

To make the overnight oats, combine the milk, peanut butter and maple syrup (if using) in a medium lidded container. Gently whisk the ingredients together. Add the oats and mix again, ensuring that all of the oats are submerged in the liquid. Cover the container and refrigerate the oats for 6 hours or overnight.

To make the chia jam, place the raspberries in a small lidded container. Mash the raspberries well with a fork. Add the chia seeds and mix until they are combined with the raspberries. Cover the container and refrigerate the chia jam for 6 hours or overnight.

The next day, uncover both the oats and the chia jam and stir each of them thoroughly. If your oats are thicker than you'd like, you can thin them with a little more milk.

Transfer the oats to bowls. Add dollops of the chia jam (no more than 2 tablespoons [30 g] for babies 6 to 12 months), and swirl the jam throughout the oats. Sprinkle each serving with the nuts (if using) and serve with the sliced bananas. Early eaters will love eating oatmeal with their hands and will have great fun scooping it out and spreading it on the high chair. You can encourage them to self-feed by preloading the oatmeal onto two or three spoons at a time for them to practice with.

Store leftover oatmeal and chia jam in airtight containers in the refrigerator for up to 3 days. Leftover chia jam can be frozen for up to 3 months.

COOK'S TIP: Double the chia jam ingredients for a nutritious sweet spread for toast and muffins, or to naturally sweeten yogurt and oatmeal.

Prep Time:
6 minutes

Chill Time:
6 hours or overnight

Yield:
Serves 2 adults + 2 children

MAKE-AHEAD

FREEZER FRIENDLY

VEGAN OPTION

DAIRY-FREE OPTION

EGG FREE

SOURCE OF IRON & FIBER

MESSY MEAL

Herby Hummus Dip

Hummus is a fantastic first food for babies! Not only is it packed full of iron and protein, but it is also incredibly easy to incorporate into your baby's everyday meals and snacks. I like to whip up a batch once a week to have on hand to use as a spread or dip, to mix through pasta or to jazz up sandwiches and wraps.

What I love most about traditional hummus is that it has such distinct flavor but is still mild enough to marry well with most other foods. To switch things up, I like to add fresh herbs, which give the hummus an additional layer of delicate-yet-punchy freshness while preserving that familiar warmth and comfort that we all know and love. If you want to alternate, you can easily strip down this recipe to make traditional hummus by omitting the herbs altogether and following the same method detailed in the directions.

1 (15-oz [400-g]) can chickpeas, drained and rinsed

¼ cup (60 g) tahini

2 tbsp (30 ml) extra virgin olive oil

Juice of 1 medium lemon

1 small clove garlic, or as needed

½ tsp ground cumin

Black pepper, as needed

2 tbsp (30 ml) water, plus more as needed

½ cup (30 g) roughly chopped fresh parsley

¼ cup (10 g) roughly chopped fresh basil

2 tbsp (6 g) roughly chopped fresh chives

Salt, as needed (optional, for kids 12+ months)

In a blender or food processor, combine the chickpeas, tahini, oil, lemon juice, garlic, cumin, black pepper and water. Blend the ingredients on high speed for 1 minute. Remove the blender's lid and scrape down the sides of the jar, then blend the mixture again for 1 minute.

Add the parsley, basil and chives to the blender and blend the ingredients again, adding more water, 1 tablespoon (15 ml) at a time, if needed. The hummus is ready once the herbs are completely blended and the consistency is smooth. Taste the hummus for seasoning and add the salt (if using).

To serve the hummus, you can spread it on toast, use it as a spread in wraps or sandwiches, serve it as a dip for soft vegetable sticks, spoon it onto a baked potato or mix it through cooked pasta.

Store the hummus in an airtight container in the refrigerator for up to 4 days. The hummus will likely firm up after being chilled, in which case you will need to mix in a little water to loosen up the consistency before serving it. To freeze the hummus, divide it into individual portions and freeze them for up to 3 months. Thaw the hummus in the refrigerator or at room temperature.

NUTRITIONIST'S TIP: Tahini and chickpeas are both great sources of iron. Serving these ingredients as hummus is one of the easiest ways to give them to babies!

Prep Time:
6 minutes

Cook Time:
None

Yield:
1½ cups (360 g)

30 MINUTES OR LESS

MAKE-AHEAD

FREEZER FRIENDLY

VEGAN

DAIRY FREE

EGG FREE

NUT FREE

SOURCE OF IRON & PROTEIN

Mixed Bean Burgers

If you're looking for a baby-friendly alternative to beef burgers, then look no further. Packed full of iron, protein and fiber, these flavorful burgers are soft enough for younger babies to gum while still maintaining a firm enough texture so that you aren't left with a mushy patty. My kids are longtime burger enthusiasts, and they absolutely love this meat-free version!

These burgers can be cooked from frozen and make for a low-effort midweek meal. I also like to serve them, minus the bun, for lunches with a sprinkle of mozzarella melted on top and some veggies on the side.

Nonstick cooking spray, as needed

1 tbsp (15 ml) avocado or olive oil

½ medium red bell pepper, diced

2 scallions, finely chopped

2 tsp (6 g) minced garlic

1 tsp ground cumin

½ tsp smoked paprika or regular paprika

1 (15-oz [400-g]) can black beans, drained and rinsed

1 (15-oz [400-g]) can chickpeas, drained and rinsed

1 tbsp (15 g) tomato paste

2 large eggs, beaten

1 cup (100 g) dried breadcrumbs

Salt, as needed (optional, for kids 12+ months)

Black pepper, as needed

Toasted burger buns and toppings of choice, for serving

Preheat the oven to 375°F (190°C, gas mark 5). Line a large baking sheet with parchment paper and spray the paper with the nonstick cooking spray.

Heat a small frying pan over medium-high heat and add the oil. Once the oil is hot, add the bell pepper and sauté it for 2 minutes. Add the scallions, garlic, cumin and smoked paprika. Sauté the mixture for 1 minute, until it is fragrant. Turn off the heat and set the frying pan aside.

In a food processor, combine the black beans and chickpeas. Process the beans on low speed for 10 to 20 seconds to break them down—do not overprocess the beans, as they need to still have texture. Overprocessed beans will result in mushy burgers.

Transfer the beans to a large bowl. Add the bell pepper mixture, tomato paste, eggs, breadcrumbs, salt (if using) and black pepper. Mix the ingredients together until everything is well combined. Form the mixture into burgers using ⅓ cup (80 g) of the mixture for each patty. Arrange the patties on the prepared baking sheet. Bake the patties for 10 to 12 minutes on each side, or until they reach your desired crispiness.

To serve the burgers, cut them into strips for early eaters or into bite-sized pieces for babies working on their pincer grasp and serve them as deconstructed burgers. For older kids and adults, serve the patties with the toasted burger buns and toppings as traditional burgers.

Store the burgers in an airtight container in the refrigerator for up to 3 days. To freeze the burgers, stack them between sheets of parchment paper in a freezer bag and freeze them for up to 3 months. To reheat frozen burgers, place them on a large baking sheet lined with parchment paper and bake them at 350°F (180°C, gas mark 4) for 15 to 20 minutes, or until they are heated through.

Prep Time:
10 minutes

Cook Time:
20 to 24 minutes

Yield:
8 burgers

MAKE-AHEAD

FREEZER FRIENDLY

LUNCHBOX FRIENDLY

VEGETARIAN

DAIRY FREE

NUT FREE

SOURCE OF IRON, PROTEIN & FIBER

TWENTY-MINUTE
Meals

Whether or not you enjoy cooking, when you are a busy parent there is rarely time on a jam-packed weeknight to make complicated dinners or to spend long periods of time babysitting food at the stove—especially if you have a baby attached to your hip or a toddler that is demanding your attention.

Over the years, I have learned that delicious and healthy meals can be quick and simple meals. When I'm feeling exhausted, there is no need to make things harder on myself by trying to prepare banquet-style spreads. There is a time and place for those kinds of meals, but a weeknight after a long day is not one of them!

In this chapter, I am sharing some of my family's favorite meals that come together in 20 minutes or less. They are not only nutritious but also appeal to all ages and are bursting with flavor. These are great recipes to rely on for when you are racing against the clock and bedtime is near. They are particularly useful when your freezer stash is running low or you have forgotten to defrost a meal for dinner—which I have done many times!

Creamy Tomato and Carrot Pasta with Steam-Roasted Broccolini

If there's one meal I can guarantee my kids will love, it's a bowl of pasta topped with this lusciously creamy tomato sauce. I love this sauce because it is not only quick and easy to whip up, but it also has a beautifully rich and silky texture. It has the added nutrition of carrots too! I like to pair this dish with steam-roasted broccolini. Cooking vegetables this way means you get all the softness of steaming and the delicious caramelized flavors of roasting!

1 lb (450 g) broccolini (see Cook's Tip)

2 tbsp (30 ml) avocado or olive oil, divided

½ tsp onion granules

Salt, as needed (optional, for kids 12+ months)

Black pepper, as needed

8 oz (230 g) chickpea or lentil pasta (such as fusilli)

½ medium yellow onion, diced

2 small carrots, grated

2 tsp (6 g) minced garlic

1 tsp dried basil

1 (15-oz [400-g]) jar passata or strained tomatoes

2 tsp (10 g) tomato paste

¼ cup (60 g) mascarpone cheese or 2 tbsp (30 g) cream cheese

Grated Cheddar cheese, for serving (optional)

COOK'S TIP: If you can't get broccolini, use regular broccoli and cut the individual florets in half to cut down the cooking time.

Bring a large pot of water to a boil over high heat. Preheat the oven to 400°F (200°C, gas mark 6).

If the broccolini stalks are thick, halve them lengthwise. Place the broccolini on a large baking sheet and add 1 tablespoon (15 ml) of the oil, the onion granules, the salt (if using) and the black pepper. Toss the ingredients together, cover the baking sheet with aluminum foil and steam roast the broccolini for 15 minutes, until it is fork-tender.

Meanwhile, add the pasta to the boiling water and cook it according to the package's instructions. Drain the pasta and set it aside.

While the pasta is cooking, heat a large frying pan over medium-high heat, and add the remaining 1 tablespoon (15 ml) of oil. Once the oil is hot, add the onion and carrots and cook them for 2 minutes, stirring often. Add the garlic and basil. Stir the mixture and cook it for 1 minute, until the garlic is fragrant.

Add the passata, tomato paste and a pinch of black pepper, and stir until the ingredients are well combined. Cook the sauce for 2 to 3 minutes, stirring constantly, until it is bubbling. Add the mascarpone cheese and stir the sauce until the cheese has melted. The sauce should be creamy.

Add the drained pasta to the sauce and mix until all of the pasta is nicely coated. Turn off the heat and stir in a pinch of salt (if using). Remove the broccolini from the oven and serve it whole alongside the pasta with a sprinkling of the Cheddar cheese (if using).

The pasta is best served freshly cooked, but leftovers can be stored in the refrigerator for up to 3 days.

Prep Time:
5 minutes

Cook Time:
15 minutes

Yield:
Serves 2 adults + 2 children

30 MINUTES OR LESS

VEGETARIAN

EGG FREE

NUT FREE

SOURCE OF IRON & PROTEIN

MESSY MEAL

Prep Time:
5 minutes

Cook Time:
15 minutes

Yield:
Serves 2 adults +
2 children

30 MINUTES OR LESS

MAKE-AHEAD

FREEZER FRIENDLY

DAIRY FREE

EGG FREE

NUT FREE

SOURCE OF IRON & PROTEIN

MESSY MEAL

Quick Chicken and Gravy

If you think you don't have time to cook a flavorful and comforting chicken stew on a busy weeknight, think again! This recipe was inspired by my kids' love for a classic Caribbean dish called brown stew chicken, which is essentially chunks of juicy chicken cooked in a rich, slightly sweet and mildly spiced gravy. Over the years, I have adapted the recipe to reduce the sodium, make it more baby friendly and, in this instance, to radically reduce the cooking time. To keep this recipe quick and simple, I recommend serving it with quick-cooking or instant rice. But it's also delicious served over creamy mashed potatoes!

1 tsp smoked paprika

1 tsp onion powder

½ tsp ground allspice (pimento; optional)

½ tsp mild chili powder

1 tsp dried thyme

1 lb (450 g) boneless, skinless chicken breast, diced

1 tbsp (15 ml) olive oil

1 small yellow onion, thinly sliced

1 small green bell pepper, cut into chunks

1 small red bell pepper, cut into chunks

1 tsp minced garlic

Black pepper, as needed

1½ cups (360 ml) low-sodium chicken stock

1 tbsp (15 ml) Worcestershire sauce

1 tbsp (15 g) tomato paste

2 (8-oz [230-g]) pouches cooked or instant white or brown rice or grain of choice, for serving

Salt, as needed (optional, for kids 12+ months)

Sliced tomato or peeled and sliced cucumber or cucumber sticks, for serving

In a small bowl, mix together the smoked paprika, onion powder, allspice, chili powder and thyme.

Place the chicken in a medium bowl and add half of the spice mixture. Stir until all of the chicken pieces are coated in the spice mixture.

Heat a large frying pan over medium-high heat and add the oil. Once the oil is hot, add the chicken in an even layer and sear it for 2 minutes on both sides.

Add the onion, green bell pepper, red bell pepper, garlic, black pepper and remaining spice mixture. Cook the chicken and vegetables for 3 minutes, stirring often.

Add the stock, Worcestershire sauce and tomato paste and stir until the ingredients are well combined. Bring the mixture to a boil, reduce the heat to medium and cook the chicken and gravy, uncovered, for 7 to 8 minutes, stirring often. If the gravy reduces too much, add a little water, but not too much.

Meanwhile, warm or cook the rice according to the package's instructions. Taste the stew for seasoning and add the salt (if using). Allow the chicken and gravy to cool before serving it with the rice. Serve the tomato or cucumber on the side. The chicken and the bell peppers are a suitable size and shape for babies of all ages, but you can cut them into smaller pieces for older babies, if you prefer. Try mixing the stew into the rice to make it easier for your baby or toddler to pick up with their hands or with a spoon.

Store any leftovers in an airtight container in the refrigerator for up to 3 days. To freeze the stew, divide the cooled stew into individual portions and freeze them for up to 3 months. Defrost the stew in the refrigerator before reheating it in a saucepan with a splash of water.

Cheats Veggie Pizza

Delicious homemade, cheesy pizza heaven without the fuss of making and rolling out your own dough or buying a pricey ready-made base: This cheats pizza made on slices of toast checks all the boxes for a nutritious, quick, tasty and kid-friendly food—and all in twenty minutes!

I prefer to use sourdough bread for this recipe, as it holds its shape well, but feel free to use whatever bread you want. And don't feel that you have to stick to the ingredient list religiously—this is the perfect opportunity to clear out your refrigerator and use up any leftover veggies as well as a chance to get toddlers involved in the kitchen by having them choose some toppings to include and assemble their own pizzas.

The sauce for this recipe is super quick and easy to put together. But if you want to save even more time and energy, you can use a premade marinara or pizza sauce. Just be sure to check labels and opt for the low-sodium and low-sugar variety.

Prep Time:
5 minutes

Cook Time:
15 minutes

Yield:
8 slices

PIZZA

8 (2½ x 5½" [6 x 14–cm], ½" [1-cm]-thick) slices sourdough bread (see Serving Tip)

½ cup (15 g) fresh baby spinach, roughly chopped

2 cups (230 g) grated mozzarella cheese

½ medium red onion, diced

½ medium red bell pepper, diced

¼ cup (40 g) canned or frozen corn (see Cook's Tip)

1 tsp dried oregano

Black pepper, as needed

Fruit of choice, for serving

TOMATO SAUCE

½ cup (120 ml) passata or strained tomatoes

¼ cup (60 g) tomato paste

½ tsp garlic granules or garlic powder

1 tsp dried oregano

To make the pizzas, preheat the broiler to medium-high. Line a large baking sheet with parchment paper.

Arrange the sourdough bread on the prepared baking sheet, and toast the bread under the broiler for 1 to 2 minutes on each side. Alternatively, you can use a toaster for this step, if you prefer.

Meanwhile, make the tomato sauce. In a medium bowl, combine the passata, tomato paste, garlic granules and oregano. Stir to combine the ingredients.

Evenly spoon the tomato sauce over each slice of toast, using the back of the spoon to spread the sauce out to the edges. Evenly distribute the spinach on each slice of toast, followed by the mozzarella cheese, onion, bell pepper and corn. Sprinkle the oregano and black pepper over the pizzas.

Place the pizzas under the broiler and cook them for 4 to 6 minutes, until the cheese is bubbly and just starting to brown. Allow the pizzas to cool sufficiently before serving. Cut them into strips for early eaters or bite-sized pieces for babies working on their pincer grasp. Alternatively, simply leave the pizzas as they are, or cut them in half for toddlers. Serve the pizzas alongside the fruit. These pizzas are best served freshly cooked.

SERVING TIP: If you are using an artisan-style bread, be sure to cut off the toasted crusts, as they would be too hard for younger babies to break down.

COOK'S TIP: If your baby is younger than 1 year, either mash the corn to make it easier to eat or omit it entirely.

30

30 MINUTES OR LESS

VEGETARIAN

NUT FREE

SOURCE OF IRON & PROTEIN

30 MINUTES OR LESS

MAKE-AHEAD

FREEZER FRIENDLY

VEGETARIAN

EGG FREE

SOURCE OF IRON

MESSY MEAL

Spinach and Almond Pesto Pasta

One of the things I love about pesto is its versatility. Not only can you play around with the formula and slip in some extra veggies, but you can also use the finished product in so many ways. Here I pair this pesto with pasta, but you can use the pesto as a dip, a spread, a replacement for pizza sauce, a topping for chicken or fish, a salad dressing or mixed through cooked grains—the possibilities are almost endless!

I have added spinach to this baby-friendly pesto to give it a boost of iron, but I do not use so much that the flavor is bitter and overpowers the fresh, slightly minty notes of basil. Your baby might make faces while eating this meal, but it doesn't mean they don't like it—it's just a flavor bomb for them, and their reactions are so fun to watch!

8 oz (230 g) pasta of choice (see Cook's Tip)

3 tbsp (20 g) grated Parmesan cheese, plus more for serving

2 cups (60 g) tightly packed fresh baby spinach

1 cup (30 g) tightly packed fresh basil

½ cup (35 g) unsalted slivered or sliced almonds

½ cup (120 ml) extra virgin olive oil

Juice of ½ medium lemon

1 small clove garlic

Black pepper, as needed

3 to 4 medium beefsteak tomatoes, cut into half-moons, wedges or slices, for serving

Bring a large pot of water to a boil over high heat. Add the pasta and cook it according to the package's instructions.

While the pasta is cooking, combine the Parmesan cheese, spinach, basil, almonds, oil, lemon juice, garlic and black pepper in a food processor or blender. Process the ingredients on high speed for 1 minute. Remove the food processor's lid and scrape down the sides of the bowl, and then process the mixture again for 1 minute, or until the pesto is well blended. The pesto is supposed to be thick, but you can add 1 tablespoon (15 ml) of water to thin the consistency, if preferred.

Drain the pasta and return it to the pot. Add the pesto to the pasta and mix them together until all of the pasta is well coated in the pesto. Top the pasta with additional Parmesan if desired. Serve the pasta with the tomatoes on the side.

If you are making the pesto ahead of time or not using it all at once, it can be stored in an airtight container in the refrigerator for up to 1 week. To freeze the pesto, divide it into individual portions and freeze them for up to 3 months. Defrost the pesto overnight in the refrigerator and add a splash of water to thin it, if necessary.

COOK'S TIP: Fusilli, rigatoni and penne are great pasta shapes for younger babies.

NUTRITIONIST'S TIP: Try a high-iron and high-protein pasta, like a chickpea- or lentil-based variety. Chickpea and lentil pastas are a baby-friendly, nutrient-dense food to help round out a meal!

Salmon and Egg Fried Rice

Chinese takeout is a favorite for many of us, but the dishes are often loaded with sodium and sugar, making them a not-so-baby-friendly option. As a lover of Chinese takeout, I have become accustomed to re-creating my favorite dishes at home and playing around with the ingredients to omit the sugar and reduce the salt so that babies and kids can enjoy them too. Not only is this quick recipe more nutritious than takeout, but it also makes for a nice twist on classic egg fried rice. Both adults and children will love this meal, which is not only bursting with flavor but is also loaded with veggies! Feel free to skip the salmon if you want to make this meal vegetarian. The eggs and peas will provide enough iron and protein to round out the meal.

SAUCE

1 tsp ginger paste or ½ tsp ground ginger

1 tbsp (15 ml) low-sodium soy sauce

2 tbsp (30 ml) 100% orange juice

1 tbsp (15 g) tahini

FRIED RICE

1 tbsp (15 ml) avocado or olive oil

½ medium red bell pepper, cut into ¼" (6-mm)-thick strips

½ cup (110 g) baby corn, halved lengthwise

2 to 3 scallions, thinly sliced

2 tsp (6 g) minced garlic

¼ cup (25 g) grated carrots

1 cup (65 g) snow peas

⅓ cup (45 g) frozen peas

2 (8-oz [230-g]) pouches cooked or instant white or brown rice, preferably chilled

2 large eggs

1 (6-oz [170-g]) can flaked salmon, drained or 1 cup (130 g) leftover flaked cooked salmon

Black pepper, as needed

Salt, as needed (optional, for kids 12+ months)

To make the sauce, mix together the ginger paste, soy sauce, orange juice and tahini in a small bowl. Set the sauce aside.

Heat a large wok or frying pan over medium-high heat and add the oil. Once the oil is hot, add the bell pepper and baby corn, and sauté them for 2 minutes.

Add the scallions, garlic, carrots and snow peas. Mix the vegetables well and sauté them for 2 minutes, stirring often. Add the frozen peas and the rice. Stir everything together and cook the mixture for 3 minutes, stirring often.

Reduce the heat to medium. Using a spatula, move the rice and vegetable mixture to one side of the wok and crack the eggs into the open space. Gently scramble the eggs in a circular motion for about 2 minutes, until they are cooked, then mix everything together.

Whisk the sauce again to redistribute the ingredients. Add the sauce to the wok, then add the salmon and black pepper. Stir to thoroughly combine the ingredients. Cook the fried rice for 2 minutes, stirring often, until the salmon is warmed through. Taste the fried rice for seasoning and add the salt (if using).

Serve the fried rice on a lipped plate or in a bowl. You can cut larger pieces of food into bite-sized pieces for older babies, or you can leave everything as it is, as there is a variety of shapes and sizes for babies to try. Your baby may only suck or gnaw on the baby corn and snow peas at first, and this is totally fine—they will still get to explore by tasting the flavors and experiencing the different textures.

The fried rice can be stored in an airtight container in the refrigerator for up to 3 days. Reheat the fried rice in a wok or frying pan with ½ tablespoon (8 ml) of avocado or olive oil over medium heat.

Prep Time:
5 minutes

Cook Time:
15 minutes

Yield:
Serves 2 adults + 2 children

30 MINUTES OR LESS

MAKE-AHEAD

DAIRY FREE

NUT FREE

SOURCE OF IRON & PROTEIN

MESSY MEAL

Prep Time:
5 minutes

Cook Time:
15 minutes

Yield:
Serves 2 adults +
2 children

Garlic Butter Shrimp Spaghetti and Steam-Roasted Green Beans

I have a bit of a weakness for the wonderful combination that is garlic and butter, and this super quick meal hits the spot perfectly! Juicy sautéed shrimp bathed in a garlicky, buttery and slightly lemony sauce, then tossed through spaghetti—this is one of those meals that pleases both adults and kids without compromising on flavor. Often, parents assume they shouldn't include much butter in their kids' food, but fats like butter—especially grass-fed butter—are an important part of a balanced diet for babies and kids. They support brain and nervous system development, and they help kids feel satisfied after a meal.

1 lb (450 g) fresh slender green beans

2 tsp (6 g) onion granules or onion powder, divided

1 tbsp (15 ml) avocado or olive oil

Salt, as needed (optional, for kids 12+ months)

8 oz (230 g) chickpea or lentil spaghetti (other shapes of pasta work too)

10 oz (300 g) large peeled and deveined raw shrimp or prawns

1 tsp Old Bay Seasoning or smoked paprika

3 tbsp (45 g) unsalted butter

3 tsp (9 g) minced garlic

Juice of ½ medium lemon

3 tbsp (9 g) finely chopped fresh parsley

Black pepper, as needed

Grated Parmesan cheese, for serving (optional)

Bring a large pot of water to a boil over high heat. Preheat the oven to 400°F (200°C, gas mark 6).

Place the green beans on a large baking sheet. Top the green beans with 1 teaspoon of the onion granules, the oil and salt (if using). Toss everything together, cover the baking sheet with aluminum foil and steam roast the green beans for 15 minutes, until they are fork-tender.

Meanwhile, add the spaghetti to the boiling water and cook it according to the package's instructions. Drain the spaghetti and set it aside.

While the pasta is cooking, place the shrimp in a small bowl. Sprinkle the remaining 1 teaspoon of onion granules and the Old Bay Seasoning over the shrimp, then mix to coat the shrimp in the seasonings. Heat a large frying pan over medium heat and add the butter. Once the butter has melted, add the garlic and cook it for 30 seconds , stirring often. Add the shrimp in an even layer and cook them for 2 minutes on each side, until they are pink.

Add the lemon juice and deglaze the frying pan for 30 seconds, using a wooden spoon to mix everything together and loosen up any brown bits stuck to the bottom. Reduce the heat to low. Add the parsley, black pepper and spaghetti. Use tongs to toss the spaghetti and shrimp in the garlic butter sauce. Add some additional salt (if using) and toss again.

Serve the green beans alongside the pasta with a sprinkling of Parmesan cheese (if using). For younger babies, chop the shrimp into small pieces and mix them throughout their serving of pasta. Some babies may only suck on a whole piece of shrimp, so chopping the shrimp will make eating easier.

This dish is best served freshly cooked, but leftovers can be stored in the refrigerator for up to 3 days.

Oven-Baked Cod and Asparagus with Garlic Buttered Toast

Cod is a delicate fish that is incredibly soft and flaky, which makes it a great option for babies and toddlers. Often referred to as the "chicken of the sea," cod has a mild taste that tends to appeal to small kids—and adults—who are still learning to like fish.

What I love most about cod is how quickly it cooks—I can whip up a nutritious meal in no time at all. For this dish, I like to make things even simpler by baking the fish right alongside the asparagus on a baking sheet. This is a light, fresh meal that leaves behind delicious juices that can be mopped up with the garlic buttered toast!

4 (1" [2.5-cm]-thick) skinless cod fillets or other mild white fish

1 (8-oz [230-g]) bunch fresh asparagus

2 tbsp (30 ml) avocado or olive oil

Juice of ½ medium lemon

½ tsp Old Bay Seasoning or Cajun seasoning, or more to taste

1 tsp minced garlic

1½ tsp (2 g) dried parsley or 1½ tbsp (5 g) finely chopped fresh parsley, divided

Black pepper, as needed

Salt, as needed (optional, for kids 12+ months)

⅓ cup (75 g) softened butter

½ tsp garlic granules or garlic powder, or more to taste

1 small French baguette, cut in ½" to 1" (1- to 2.5-cm)-thick slices

Preheat the oven to 400°F (200°C, gas mark 6). Line a large baking sheet with parchment paper. Arrange the cod fillets and asparagus next to each other on the prepared baking sheet.

In a small bowl, combine the oil, lemon juice, Old Bay Seasoning, garlic and 1 teaspoon of the dried parsley or 1 tablespoon (3 g) of the fresh parsley. Drizzle the mixture evenly over the cod and asparagus, and season with black pepper and salt (if using). Bake the cod and asparagus for 10 to 12 minutes, or until the asparagus is soft and the cod flakes easily with a fork.

Meanwhile, in a small bowl, mix together the butter, garlic granules, the remaining ½ teaspoon of dried parsley or ½ tablespoon (2 g) of fresh parsley and black pepper. Set the garlic butter aside.

Toast the slices of baguette for 2 to 3 minutes, or until they are golden. Top each slice of toast evenly with the garlic butter.

Allow the cod and asparagus to rest until it is cool enough to handle, then serve them alongside the garlic buttered toast. For younger babies, cut the garlic toast into strips and use a fork to break the fish into large chunks to make it easier for them to pick up and hold. For older babies working on their pincer grasp, you can flake the fish for them instead. If the asparagus spears are more than ¼ inch (6 mm) thick, be sure to slice them in half lengthwise before serving.

Store the cod and asparagus in an airtight container in the refrigerator for up to 3 days. Reheat them, covered, in the oven at 350°F (180°C, gas mark 4) for 10 to 15 minutes, or until they are heated through.

Prep Time:
8 minutes

Cook Time:
10 to 12 minutes

Yield:
Serve 2 adults + 2 children

30
30 MINUTES OR LESS

EGG FREE

NUT FREE

SOURCE OF IRON & PROTEIN

Prep Time:
5 minutes

Cook Time:
15 minutes

Yield:
**Serves 2 adults +
2 children**

**30 MINUTES OR
LESS**

VEGETARIAN

EGG FREE

NUT FREE

**SOURCE OF IRON
& PROTEIN**

MESSY MEAL

Creamy Ricotta and Pea Pasta

A healthier take on mac and cheese, this is a quick and simple pasta dish that strikes a delectable balance between being light and fresh and comforting and satisfying. The trick to preventing the creamy sauce from being too heavy is to use a whisk to whip the ricotta with the milk before adding it to the pan. I just love the lightness that this step brings to the dish, and along with the slight zing from the lemon, the flavors balance perfectly.

You can use any pasta you like for this dish, but for younger babies I recommend using an easy-to-hold variety such as fusilli, rigatoni and penne. Note that it's the peas that add the iron here—if you decide to use a different veggie, be sure to use a chickpea or lentil pasta, or add an iron-rich food on the side.

8 oz (230 g) pasta of choice
(see Nutritionist's Tip)

1 cup (250 g) full-fat ricotta
cheese

¼ cup (60 ml) full-fat milk

1 tsp onion granules or onion
powder

½ tbsp (8 ml) avocado or
olive oil

1 tsp minced garlic

Zest of 1 small lemon

Black pepper, as needed

1 cup (135 g) frozen peas

⅓ cup (35 g) grated
Parmesan cheese

Salt, as needed (optional, for
kids 12+ months)

Fruit of choice, for serving

Bring a large pot of water to a boil over high heat. Add the pasta and cook it according to the package's instructions. Before draining the pasta, reserve ⅓ cup (80 ml) of the starchy pasta water. Set the drained pasta and reserved water aside.

While the pasta is cooking, combine the ricotta cheese, milk and onion granules in a medium bowl. Whisk the ingredients until they are completely smooth.

Heat a large frying pan over medium heat and add the oil. Once the oil is hot, add the garlic and cook it for 30 seconds, until it is fragrant. Add the ricotta cheese mixture, reserved pasta water, lemon zest and black pepper. Whisk until the ingredients are well combined.

Once the sauce starts to bubble, add the peas. Cook the peas for 1 minute, then add the pasta and toss everything together.

Add the Parmesan cheese and stir it into the sauce until it is melted. Taste the pasta for seasoning and add the salt (if using).

Allow the pasta to cool slightly before serving it with some fresh fruit on the side. This dish is best served freshly cooked.

NUTRITIONIST'S TIP: Pasta can be a sneaky source of iron! You can find enriched whole wheat, chickpea or lentil pastas in most stores. All of these tend to have decent amounts of iron per serving.

Lentil and Spinach Dahl with Naan

This dahl recipe is my simple go-to option whenever my family gets cravings for those deep, warming and aromatic flavors of Indian food. The coconut milk gives the dish such beautiful depth of flavor and provides some creamy comfort, which leaves you feeling fully satisfied after your meal.

Generally speaking, dahl isn't a complicated meal to make, but I find that using precooked or instant lentils shaves off a good fifteen minutes of cooking time, which makes a world of difference when I'm feeling tired and unmotivated! We like to eat dahl with fluffy naan bread, but if you want to bulk up the meal, you can serve it with rice too.

1 tbsp (15 ml) avocado or olive oil

½ medium yellow onion, diced

2 tsp (6 g) minced garlic

1 cup (110 g) shredded carrots

1 tbsp (9 g) mild curry powder

1 tsp ground turmeric (see Good to Know tip)

1 tsp ground cumin

Black pepper, as needed

14 oz (400 g) precooked or instant green or brown lentils, rinsed

1 (15-oz [400-g]) can crushed or chopped tomatoes, undrained

1 (14-oz [400-ml]) can full-fat coconut milk

4 medium or large store-bought naan breads

4 cups (120 g) loosely packed fresh baby spinach

Salt, as needed (optional, for kids 12+ months)

Sliced or cubed avocado, for serving

Heat a large frying pan or pot over medium-high heat and add the oil. Once the oil is hot, add the onion and cook it for 2 minutes. Add the garlic, carrots, curry powder, turmeric, cumin and black pepper. Mix the ingredients together well. Cook the mixture for 2 minutes, stirring constantly, until the garlic is fragrant.

Add the lentils, tomatoes and coconut milk and stir to combine the ingredients. Bring the mixture to a boil, then reduce the heat to medium. Simmer the lentils, uncovered, for 7 to 8 minutes, stirring often.

Meanwhile, heat up the naan breads according to the package's instructions.

Add the baby spinach to the lentils and stir to combine. Simmer the dahl for 2 minutes, or until the spinach is wilted. Taste the dahl for seasoning and add the salt (if using).

To make it easier for younger babies to eat, spread the cooled dahl on strips of the naan bread. Older babies and toddlers may prefer to dip their naan into the dahl or use a spoon or their fingers to scoop it up. Serve the dahl with the avocado on the side.

Store the dahl in an airtight container in the refrigerator for up to 3 days. To freeze the dahl, divide the cooled dahl into individual portions and freeze them for up to 3 months. Defrost the dahl overnight in the refrigerator before reheating it, or gently reheat frozen dahl on the stove with a splash of water.

GOOD TO KNOW: Turmeric may stain bamboo or silicone tableware as well as clothing, so be sure that baby is wearing a full-sleeved bib or is shirtless. Wash plates and cutlery with warm soapy water right after eating.

Prep Time:
3 minutes

Cook Time:
15 minutes

Yield:
Serves 2 adults + 2 children

30 MINUTES OR LESS

MAKE-AHEAD

FREEZER FRIENDLY

VEGETARIAN

NUT FREE

SOURCE OF IRON, PROTEIN & FIBER

MESSY MEAL

Prep Time:
6 minutes

Cook Time:
6 to 8 minutes

Yield:
Serves 1 adult + 2 children

30 MINUTES OR LESS

VEGETARIAN

EGG FREE

NUT FREE

SOURCE OF IRON, PROTEIN & FIBER

Avocado, Black Bean and Mozzarella Quesadillas

Quesadillas make a speedy, no-fuss meal and are an absolute must for those busy weeknights. There are so many options when it comes to fillings, and this recipe is one that strikes a great balance between being nutritious for babies and kids and bursting with enough flavor to keep the adults happy too.

Packed with iron, protein and fiber from the black beans, healthy fats from the avocado and comforting gooey mozzarella, these quesadillas are substantial enough to serve for an evening meal and will leave everyone feeling satisfied and well fed. If you would like to make this into a complete meal for two adults and two kids, simply make an extra quesadilla or two in an additional frying pan.

2 medium avocados

1 tsp fresh lime juice

½ tsp garlic granules or garlic powder

½ tsp smoked paprika

Black pepper, as needed

Salt, as needed (optional, for kids 12+ months)

⅔ cup (115 g) canned black beans, drained and rinsed

2 large whole wheat or white-flour tortillas

⅔ cup (75 g) grated mozzarella cheese, divided

1 tbsp (15 ml) avocado or olive oil

1 cup (260 g) store-bought fresh salsa, for serving

Fruit of choice, for serving

In a small bowl, mash the avocados. Add the lime juice, garlic granules, smoked paprika, black pepper and salt (if using). Mix the ingredients well.

On a plate, lightly mash the black beans with a fork. Add the beans to the avocado mixture. Mix again until the ingredients are well combined.

Place a tortilla on a plate and place half of the avocado and bean mixture on one side of the tortilla. Sprinkle ⅓ cup (40 g) of the mozzarella cheese over the avocado and bean mixture. Fold the tortilla over. Repeat this process with the remaining tortilla.

Heat a large nonstick frying pan over medium heat and add the oil. Once the oil is hot, add both of the folded quesadillas and cook them for 3 to 4 minutes, until the undersides are golden. Carefully flip the quesadillas and cook the other sides for 3 to 4 minutes, until the quesadillas are golden and crispy and the mozzarella is melted and gooey.

Allow the quesadillas to cool before serving them with the salsa for dipping and some fresh fruit on the side. Cut the quesadillas into slices approximately the width of two adult fingers for both younger and older babies—avoid cutting them any smaller to avoid their falling apart when picked up.

These quesadillas are best eaten right after cooking, but leftovers can be stored in an airtight container in the refrigerator for up to 2 days. Reheat the quesadillas in a hot frying pan with a splash of oil.

COOK'S TIP: This is a great recipe to load up on veggies; try adding shredded carrots, bell pepper or spinach!

ONE-POT *and* SHEET-PAN
Meals

The main appeal of one-pot and sheet-pan meals is pretty self-explanatory: You dump everything in a pot or on a baking sheet, cook the dish all in one place and save yourself the hassle of washing several pots, pans and roasting trays. I think most of us can agree that the last thing we want to do after enjoying a delicious meal is spend even more time in the kitchen clearing everything away—no thank you!

But the one-pot or sheet-pan meal is not just a tool to reduce housework. These dishes are also an easy, simple, fuss-free way of incorporating variety into your meals. Cooking everything together means you follow fewer steps than you would creating separate sides, which is great if you don't particularly enjoy cooking and would rather get things over and done with.

In this chapter, you'll find a variety of tasty recipes that explore a range of flavors and textures while simultaneously keeping mealtimes simple yet interesting—without your having to turn your kitchen upside down!

Orange and Strawberry Sheet-Pan Pancakes

As someone with pancake-obsessed kids, I think sheet-pan pancakes have to be the smartest invention yet! You get all of the fluffy yumminess of traditionally made pancakes but in a fraction of the time and with minimal effort. Say goodbye to the chore of standing at the stove flipping pancakes—all you have to do for this recipe is whip up the batter, pour it into the sheet pan and bake it in the oven. That's it!

Adding orange to these pancakes produces a light, zesty flavor as well as a subtle sweetness that perfectly complements the strawberries. Feel free to use any chopped berries you want; just be careful not to add more than 1 cup (150 g), or you'll run the risk of soggy pancakes.

Nonstick cooking spray, as needed

2 large eggs

1½ cups (360 ml) full-fat cow's milk

Zest of 1 medium orange

¼ cup (60 ml) fresh orange juice

1 tsp pure vanilla extract

2 tbsp (30 ml) melted unsalted butter

2 cups (250 g) all-purpose flour

1 tbsp (15 g) baking powder

¼ tsp salt (optional, for kids 12+ months)

1 cup (160 g) thinly sliced fresh strawberries

Pure maple syrup, for serving (optional)

Full-fat plain Greek or natural yogurt, for serving

Hemp seeds, for serving

Preheat the oven to 425°F (220°C, gas mark 7). Line a rimmed 15 x 11-inch (38 x 28-cm) baking sheet with parchment paper. It's important to use this size, since using a baking sheet that's bigger or smaller may produce different results in the pancake's final texture. Spray the parchment paper with the nonstick cooking spray.

In a large bowl, combine the eggs, milk, orange zest, orange juice, vanilla and butter. Whisk the ingredients until they are smooth.

In a medium bowl, mix together the flour, baking powder and salt (if using). Add the flour mixture to the egg mixture. Whisk until a smooth batter forms. Set the batter aside to rest for 5 minutes.

Pour the batter on the prepared baking sheet. Spread the batter out to the edges of the baking sheet. Arrange the strawberries on top of the batter. Bake the pancake for 14 to 16 minutes, or until it is slightly golden and spongy.

If you prefer a more browned pancake, you can broil the pancake for 2 minutes after baking it.

Allow the pancake to rest until it is cool enough to handle, then slice it into strips or squares. Serve the pancakes with the maple syrup (if using), a dollop of the yogurt and a sprinkling of hemp seeds for iron.

Store the pancakes in an airtight container in the refrigerator for up to 3 days. To freeze the pancakes, stack them between sheets of parchment paper in a freezer bag and freeze them for up to 3 months. To reheat, place frozen pancakes on a baking sheet, cover with aluminum foil and heat in the oven at 350°F (180°C, gas mark 4) for 10 to 15 minutes, until they are warm and soft.

Prep Time:
5 minutes +
5 minutes to rest

Cook Time:
14 to 16 minutes

Yield:
Serves 3 adults +
3 children

30 MINUTES OR LESS

MAKE-AHEAD

FREEZER FRIENDLY

LUNCHBOX FRIENDLY

VEGETARIAN

NUT FREE

Prep Time:
5 minutes

Cook Time:
35 to 40 minutes

Yield:
Serves 3 adults + 3 children

MAKE-AHEAD

FREEZER FRIENDLY

DAIRY FREE

EGG FREE

NUT FREE

SOURCE OF IRON & PROTEIN

MESSY MEAL

Chunky Chicken Soup

Many years ago, I worked in a small countryside town in Jamaica. During my time there, I learned to cook many authentic Jamaican dishes. One of my favorites is a popular dish called Saturday soup, which is a deliciously thick, hearty soup made with chicken and chunky root vegetables and infused with thyme, warming spices and the slightly sweet flavor of pumpkin. It makes a great baby-friendly soup. What I love most about this soup is just how easily it all comes together. Simply dump everything in the pot, and it takes care of itself. Canned pumpkin helps provide body and thickness without requiring the soup to boil for hours. But don't worry—while the pumpkin provides a slight sweetness, your soup will not taste like pumpkin pie!

3 cups (720 ml) low-sodium chicken stock

5 cups (1.2 L) water

1 medium leek, thickly sliced

2 medium ears of corn, quartered

1 tbsp (9 g) minced garlic

1 tsp ground allspice (pimento; optional)

1 tsp ground cumin

1 tsp mild curry powder

2 tsp (6 g) smoked paprika

4 sprigs fresh thyme or 1 tsp dried thyme

Black pepper, as needed

1 (15-oz [425-g]) can 100% pumpkin puree

1¼ lb (550 g) boneless, skinless chicken thighs, quartered

2 to 3 large yellow potatoes, cut into 2" (5-cm) pieces

3 medium carrots, peeled and thickly sliced

Salt, as needed (optional, for kids 12+ months)

Combine the stock and water in a very large pot over high heat and bring the liquid to a boil.

Once the liquid comes to a boil, reduce the heat to medium-high. Add the leek, corn, garlic, allspice, cumin, curry powder, smoked paprika, thyme and black pepper to the pot. Stir the ingredients together and cook them for 5 minutes.

Add the pumpkin and stir to combine it with the other ingredients. Add the chicken thighs, potatoes and carrots. Mix everything together and bring the soup to a boil. Reduce the heat to medium-low, cover the pot with a lid and simmer the soup for 25 to 30 minutes, stirring occasionally and adding more water if needed. The soup is ready when the liquid has thickened and the potatoes and carrots are fork-tender.

Taste the soup for seasoning and add the salt (if using). Allow the soup to cool sufficiently before serving it to your child in a bowl. Thick and chunky soups are great for early eaters—you can encourage your baby to use cutlery by preloading a spoon with soup and letting them practice self-feeding. For babies working on their pincer grasp, you can cut the larger chunks of potatoes and carrots into bite-sized pieces.

Store the soup in an airtight container in the refrigerator for up to 3 days. To freeze the soup, divide the cooled soup into individual portions and freeze them for up to 3 months. Thaw the soup in the refrigerator before reheating, or gently reheat it on the stove from frozen with a splash of water.

NUTRITIONIST'S TIP: Corn on the cob can be a fun, safe way to serve corn to your baby! No need for teeth—your baby can use their gums to gnaw off the corn kernels. This results in broken and smashed kernels, which are not choking hazards for babies younger than 1 year.

Steak and Potato Dinner Hash

Traditional breakfast hash gets a dinnertime makeover with this nutritious and mouthwatering one-pot meal. I recommend using small baby potatoes, as they cook quickly and the thin skins mean they don't need to be peeled beforehand. The steak, which is the star of the show, does a brilliant job of carrying its deep, distinctive flavors throughout all the components of the dish. You can change up the herbs and spices if you wish, and feel free to switch out the veggies for what you have on hand—just be sure to pick vegetables that cook quickly, as they aren't added until the last few minutes of cooking.

1 tsp garlic granules or garlic powder

1 tsp onion granules or onion powder

1 tbsp (3 g) Italian seasoning

Black pepper, as needed

2 (8-oz [230-g], 1" [2.5-cm]-thick) sirloin, rib eye or rump steaks

2 tbsp (30 ml) avocado or olive oil, plus more as needed

2 tsp (6 g) minced garlic

1 lb (450 g) small yellow baby potatoes, quartered lengthwise (see Cook's Tip)

1 large zucchini, sliced into half-moons

1 large red bell pepper, cut into large chunks

8 oz (230 g) fresh green beans, trimmed

Salt, as needed (optional, for kids 12+ months)

In a small bowl, mix together the garlic granules, onion granules, Italian seasoning and black pepper. Use half of the spice mixture to season the steaks on both sides.

Heat a large nonstick frying pan over medium-high heat and add the oil. Once the oil is hot, add both steaks and fry them for 4 to 5 minutes on each side, or until the outside has developed a deep brown crust and the internal temperature reaches 145°F (63°C). Transfer the steaks to a plate and cover them with aluminum foil.

Reduce the heat to medium and add a little more oil if needed. Add the garlic and cook it for 30 seconds. Add the potatoes and the remaining spice mixture. Stir the potatoes to thoroughly coat them in the spice mixture. Sauté the potatoes for 3 to 4 minutes, stirring often so they don't stick to the frying pan. Reduce the heat to low, cover the frying pan and cook the potatoes for 10 minutes, stirring them halfway through the cooking time.

Add the zucchini, bell pepper and green beans. Cook the vegetables, uncovered, for 6 to 8 minutes, stirring often, until the potatoes and vegetables are fork-tender. Turn off the heat. Taste the hash for seasoning and add the salt (if using).

Place the steaks on a cutting board and slice them into strips, or cut them into bite-sized pieces. Serve the steak with the potato hash, cutting everything into bite-sized pieces for babies working on their pincer grasp. Younger babies will likely just suck the juices from the strips of steak, which is fine—they will still get iron from those juices.

Store the steak and hash in an airtight container in the refrigerator for up to 3 days. Reheat the hash, covered, in the oven at 375°F (190°C, gas mark 5) for 10 to 15 minutes, or until it is heated through.

Prep Time:
5 minutes

Cook Time:
30 to 35 minutes

Yield:
Serves 2 adults + 2 children

DAIRY FREE

EGG FREE

NUT FREE

SOURCE OF IRON & PROTEIN

Sheet-Pan Chicken Fajitas

Sheet-pan fajitas make a fantastic low-effort weeknight meal. Seasoned with classic Mexican flavors, all you have to do is load the chicken and veggies on the baking sheet and let the oven do the work!

For smaller babies, it's best to serve deconstructed fajitas by serving each component of the wrap separately. This makes for easy self-feeding and allows baby to explore the different textures individually. For toddlers, you can slice up a wrap or serve it whole—or better yet, get them involved in putting it together and choosing which fillings they would like to add. Getting toddlers involved in making their meals is a great way to familiarize them with different foods and encourage them to try new things.

FAJITAS

2 large boneless, skinless chicken breasts, cut into ½" (1-cm)-thick strips

1 medium red bell pepper, cut into ¼" (6-mm)-thick strips

1 medium yellow bell pepper, cut into ¼" (6-mm)-thick strips

1 large red onion, cut into ¼" (6-mm)-thick strips

Juice of 1 medium lime

1 tsp garlic granules or garlic powder

1 tsp smoked paprika or regular paprika

2 tsp (2 g) dried oregano

1 tsp ground cumin

½ tsp mild chili powder (optional)

Salt, as needed (optional, for kids 12+ months)

Black pepper, as needed

1½ tbsp (20 ml) avocado or olive oil

4 large whole-grain or white-flour tortillas

FOR SERVING

1 large avocado, sliced into the desired thickness (optional)

Grated Cheddar cheese, as needed (optional)

Sour cream, as needed (optional)

Homemade or store-bought mild fresh salsa, as needed (optional)

To make the fajitas, preheat the oven to 400°F (200°C, gas mark 6). In a large bowl, combine the chicken, red bell pepper, yellow bell pepper, onion, lime juice, garlic granules, smoked paprika, oregano, cumin, chili powder (if using), salt (if using), black pepper and oil. Mix the ingredients until everything is well coated.

Spread the chicken, bell peppers and onion on a large baking sheet. Arrange the chicken and vegetables in an even layer, making sure that none of the chicken strips are overlapping. Cook the fajitas for 20 to 25 minutes, stirring the chicken and vegetables halfway through the cooking time, until the chicken is cooked through (internal temperature of 165°F [74°C]).

Serve the fajitas with the tortillas, avocado (if using), Cheddar cheese (if using), sour cream (if using) and salsa (if using). Refer to the headnote for age-appropriate serving recommendations.

The fajitas can be stored in an airtight container in the refrigerator for up to 3 days. Gently reheat the fajitas by adding the chicken, bell peppers and onions to a large nonstick frying pan with a splash of oil to prevent the chicken strips from becoming too dry.

Baby-Friendly Buddha Bowl

Buddha bowls are a fantastic way to add variety and color to your meal plan. At a glance, these bowls of goodness may appear to be complicated and fiddly, but they are actually easy to put together and a great way to use up your veggies. What's more, they can be super interactive: Toddlers love to build their own bowls and have great fun making rainbows out of food.

To keep these bowls baby friendly, make sure that everything is cooked softly and is fairly easy for your child to pick up and hold. With that said, it's a good idea to include some smaller pieces of food so that baby can work on their pincer grasp.

½ tsp ground cumin

½ tsp garlic granules or garlic powder

½ tsp onion granules or onion powder

Black pepper, as needed

2 tbsp (30 ml) avocado or olive oil

2 medium sweet potatoes, peeled and cut into ½" to ¾" (1- to 2-cm) chunks or sticks

2 cups (200 g) fresh Brussels sprouts, halved

1 cup (160 g) canned corn, drained and rinsed

1 cup (150 g) cherry or grape tomatoes, halved lengthwise

Salt, as needed (optional, for kids 12+ months)

2 large avocados, sliced or cubed into the desired size

1 cup (170 g) low-sodium, vacuum-packed cooked beets, sliced or cubed into the desired size

1 cup (240 g) store-bought hummus or Herby Hummus Dip (page 70), for serving

Preheat the oven to 400°F (200°C, gas mark 6).

In a small bowl, mix together the cumin, garlic granules, onion granules, black pepper and oil.

On a large baking sheet, arrange the sweet potato pieces and Brussels sprouts next to one another. Drizzle the sweet potatoes and Brussels sprouts with the seasoned oil. Mix well to coat the sweet potatoes and Brussels sprouts, cover the baking sheet with aluminum foil and roast the mixture for 25 minutes.

Meanwhile, mash the corn if your baby is younger than 1 year old.

Remove the baking sheet from the oven, carefully remove the foil and shake the baking sheet. Add the cherry tomatoes. Roast the vegetables, uncovered, for 15 to 20 minutes, or until the sweet potatoes and Brussels sprouts are fork-tender and the tomatoes are soft. Add the salt (if using).

You are now ready to build the Buddha bowls. For younger babies and toddlers, it's easier to serve this meal in a wide bowl or on a lipped plate. Arrange the roasted vegetables, avocados and beets along the edges of the bowl or plate and place a generous dollop of the hummus in the middle (see Serving Tip).

Store the Buddha bowl components in an airtight container in the refrigerator for up to 3 days.

SERVING TIP: If your baby or toddler becomes overwhelmed with too many choices on their plate, serve a couple of options at a time, and refill their plate as needed.

Prep Time:
6 minutes

Cook Time:
40 to 45 minutes

Yield:
Serves 2 adults + 2 children

VEGAN

DAIRY FREE

EGG FREE

NUT FREE

SOURCE OF IRON, PROTEIN & FIBER

NUT FREE

**SOURCE OF IRON
& PROTEIN**

MESSY MEAL

Cheesy Beef Taco Pasta

If you love tacos, then you'll love this baby-friendly spin-off that incorporates all of those classic flavors into one comforting pot of pasta! The mozzarella helps balance the flavors in this dish, but it's the cream cheese that adds the delicious silkiness to the sauce.

I recommend using rigatoni pasta for this recipe, as it's easy for babies to pick up, but feel free to use any pasta you like. It's also worth noting that although corn kernels are considered a choking risk to babies under a year old, when cooked in this way, they become very soft and are deemed safe to serve. With that said, you can skip or substitute them with another vegetable, cut into small pieces, if preferred.

TACO SEASONING

1½ tsp (5 g) smoked paprika

1 tsp ground cumin

½ tsp mild chili powder

2 tsp (2 g) dried oregano

PASTA

1 lb (450 g) ground beef

1 medium yellow onion, diced

1 large red bell pepper, cut into ¼" (6-mm)-thick strips

2 tsp (6 g) minced garlic

Black pepper, as needed

2 cups (520 g) store-bought mild fresh salsa (see Nutritionist's Tip)

2 tbsp (30 g) tomato paste

2 cups (480 ml) low-sodium beef stock

1½ cups (200 g) frozen corn (optional; see headnote)

8 oz (230 g) rigatoni pasta

2 tbsp (30 g) cream cheese

1 cup (110 g) grated mozzarella or Cheddar cheese

Salt, as needed (optional, for kids 12+ months)

FOR SERVING

Thinly sliced scallions, as needed (optional)

Sliced or diced avocado, as needed (optional)

Sour cream, as needed (optional)

Grated mozzarella or Cheddar cheese, as needed (optional)

To make the taco seasoning, combine the smoked paprika, cumin, chili powder and oregano in a small bowl. Set the taco seasoning aside.

To make the pasta, heat a large pot over medium-high heat. Add the beef and cook it for 4 to 5 minutes, breaking it apart with a wooden spoon as it cooks, until there is no pink remaining in the meat. Transfer the beef to a plate and set it aside. Leave a thin layer of fat in the pot.

Reduce the heat to medium and add the onion and bell pepper. Sauté them for 2 to 3 minutes. Add the garlic, taco seasoning and black pepper, and stir the ingredients until they are well combined. Cook the mixture for 1 minute, until the garlic and spices are fragrant.

Transfer the beef back to the pot, then add the salsa, tomato paste, stock and corn. Mix the ingredients together and bring the mixture to a boil. Add the pasta. Stir the mixture again and cook the pasta for 15 to 20 minutes, stirring occasionally, or until the pasta is cooked and the sauce has thickened. If the sauce begins to reduce too much, add some water as needed.

(Continued)

Cheesy Beef Taco Pasta (Continued)

Take the pasta off the heat. Add the cream cheese and mozzarella cheese, and stir until they have melted into the pasta. Taste the pasta for seasoning and add the salt (if using).

Allow the pasta to cool sufficiently before serving it to your child on a lipped plate or in a bowl. Top each serving with the scallions (if using), avocado (if using), sour cream (if using) and mozzarella cheese (if using). This is a messy meal, so be sure to protect your baby's clothing with a full-sleeved smock bib, or let them go shirtless.

Store the pasta in an airtight container in the refrigerator for up to 3 days. Reheat it in a saucepan over medium heat with a splash of water.

NUTRITIONIST'S TIP: Salsa can be high in sodium. However, fresh salsa—sold in the refrigerated section of grocery stores—often has a lower sodium content than canned or jarred varieties and is an easy way to lower sodium in your child's diet!

Mexican Chicken and Rice

If you love Mexican food, then you'll love this super easy and flavorful one-pot meal. The most work you will do here is a bit of chopping and browning the chicken. After those steps, everything more or less goes into the pot and simply requires an occasional stir. What's more, this recipe retains a good amount of moisture, which helps hold everything together and makes it easier for little hands to self-feed—it also means less mess!

SPICE BLEND

2 tsp (6 g) smoked paprika or regular paprika

2 tsp (6 g) garlic granules or garlic powder

2 tsp (6 g) onion granules or onion powder

2 tsp (2 g) dried oregano

1½ tsp (5 g) ground cumin

1 tsp mild chili powder (optional)

CHICKEN AND RICE

1 lb (450 g) boneless, skinless chicken breasts, cut into ½" (1-cm) strips or chunks

1 tbsp (15 ml) avocado or olive oil, plus more as needed

1 medium yellow onion, diced

1 medium red bell pepper, diced

1 medium green bell pepper, diced

2 tsp (6 g) minced garlic

2 tbsp (30 g) tomato paste

1 cup (260 g) homemade or store-bought mild fresh salsa

1 cup (165 g) frozen corn kernels (optional; see Cook's Tips)

2 cups (370 g) long-grain white rice (see Cook's Tips)

CHICKEN AND RICE (CONTINUED)

2 cups (480 ml) low-sodium chicken stock

Black pepper, as needed

¼ cup (12 g) finely chopped fresh cilantro (optional)

Salt, as needed (optional, for kids 12+ months)

Sliced or diced avocado, to serve (optional)

To make the spice blend, combine the smoked paprika, garlic granules, onion granules, oregano, cumin and chili powder (if using) in a small bowl. Set the bowl aside.

To make the chicken and rice, combine the chicken and half of the spice blend. Mix until all of the chicken pieces are coated in the spices. Allow the chicken to season for 5 minutes.

Heat a large frying pan over medium-high heat and add the oil. Once the oil is hot, add the chicken in an even layer, and sear it for 2 minutes on both sides. Remove the chicken from the frying pan and set it aside.

Reduce the heat to medium and return the frying pan to the heat. Add a little more oil if needed. Add the onion, red bell pepper and green bell pepper and cook them for 2 minutes, stirring often. Add the garlic, tomato paste and the remaining spice blend and mix the ingredients well. Cook the mixture for 1 minute, then add the salsa, corn (if using), rice, chicken and chicken stock. Season the mixture with black pepper and stir the ingredients well, being sure to loosen up any brown bits stuck to the frying pan.

Bring the mixture to a boil and reduce the heat to low. Cover the frying pan and cook the chicken and rice for 30 to 35 minutes, stirring occasionally to prevent the rice from sticking on the bottom of the frying pan, until the rice is tender.

(Continued)

Prep Time:
5 to 10 minutes

Cook Time:
40 to 45 minutes

Yield:
Serves 2 adults + 2 children

MAKE-AHEAD

FREEZER FRIENDLY

DAIRY FREE

EGG FREE

NUT FREE

SOURCE OF IRON & PROTEIN

Mexican Chicken and Rice (Continued)

Stir in the cilantro (if using). Taste the chicken and rice for seasoning and add salt (if using).

Allow the chicken and rice to cool sufficiently before serving it to your child on a lipped plate or in a bowl with a side of sliced avocado (if using). This is a good opportunity for baby to get some more spoon practice, as the rice will be moist and easier to scoop. Preload two or three spoons at a time for your baby to try to self-feed with, but don't worry if they are only interested in using their hands.

Store the chicken and rice in an airtight container in the refrigerator for up to 3 days. To freeze the chicken and rice, divide the cooled mixture into individual portions and freeze them for up to 3 months. Defrost the chicken and rice in the refrigerator and reheat it in a covered ovenproof dish in the oven at 375°F (190°C, gas mark 5) for 10 to 15 minutes, or until it is heated through.

COOK'S TIPS: If your baby is younger than 1 year, either mash the corn to make it easier to eat or omit it entirely.

You can use any grain you like for this dish; just be sure to adjust the cooking time accordingly.

Chicken Chow Mein

This Chinese takeout re-creation is a particular favorite of mine, as most of the components of the dish are easy for little hands to hold, and the spongy egg noodles appeal to most kids. Not only that, but it's super easy to whip up! Once you have prepped your ingredients, the dish comes together quickly and requires very little effort.

SAUCE

1 tsp ginger paste or
½ tsp ground ginger

2 tsp (10 g) tomato paste

1 tbsp (15 g) tahini

1 tbsp (15 ml) low-sodium
soy sauce

CHOW MEIN

10 oz (300 g) boneless,
skinless chicken breasts, cut
into ½" (1-cm)-thick strips

½ tsp garlic granules or
garlic powder

½ tsp onion granules or
onion powder

1 tbsp (15 ml) avocado or
olive oil

½ medium red bell pepper,
thinly sliced

½ medium green bell pepper,
thinly sliced

4 oz (120 g) slender
asparagus, woody ends
trimmed

1 cup (65 g) snow peas

1 tsp minced garlic

1 large carrot, shredded

2 scallions, thinly sliced

1 cup (100 g) bean sprouts

Black pepper, as needed

10 oz (300 g) fresh chow
mein noodles (see Cook's Tip)

Salt, as needed (optional, for
kids 12+ months)

To make the sauce, mix together the ginger paste, tomato paste, tahini and soy sauce in a small bowl. Set the sauce aside.

To make the chow mein, combine the chicken, garlic granules and onion granules in a medium bowl. Stir to thoroughly coat the chicken with the garlic and onion.

Heat a very large wok or frying pan over medium-high heat and add the oil. Once the oil is hot, add the chicken in an even layer and sear it for 2 minutes on both sides.

Reduce the heat to medium. Add the red bell pepper, green bell pepper and asparagus and cook the mixture for 2 minutes, stirring often. Add the snow peas and cook the mixture for 2 minutes, stirring often. Add the garlic, carrot, scallions and bean sprouts. Stir the ingredients together well and cook them for 2 minutes.

Add the sauce and black pepper, and stir the ingredients to thoroughly combine them. Add the noodles and use kitchen tongs to mix and toss everything together. Cook the chow mein for 2 to 3 minutes, until the noodles are warmed through. Taste the chow mein for seasoning and add salt (if using).

Allow the chow mein to cool sufficiently before serving it to your child. To make the chow mein easier for babies and toddlers to scoop up with a spoon or fork, use kitchen scissors or a knife to snip or cut the noodles into shorter pieces.

Store the chow mein in an airtight container in the refrigerator for up to 3 days. Reheat the chow mein in a frying pan over medium heat with a splash of oil.

COOK'S TIP: Fresh chow mein noodles are also known as fresh Chinese egg noodles.

Prep Time:
10 minutes

Cook Time:
15 to 20 minutes

Yield:
Serves 2 adults +
2 children

30
**30 MINUTES OR
LESS**

DAIRY FREE

NUT FREE

**SOURCE OF IRON
& PROTEIN**

Prep Time:
5 minutes

Cook Time:
35 to 45 minutes

Yield:
**Serves 2 adults +
2 children**

DAIRY FREE

EGG FREE

NUT FREE

SOURCE OF IRON

Sheet-Pan Mediterranean Salmon

This recipe was inspired by a trip we took to Turkey, where we ate at an amazing seafood restaurant that had the most succulent salmon served with a side of spiced sautéed potatoes and veggies. It was so simple and light yet so satisfying, and the kids enjoyed it too! I found that re-creating this meal on a sheet pan was the easiest approach, as it meant that I could achieve juicy salmon, crispy potatoes and tender vegetables all at once. The veggies in this meal are especially good for younger babies, as they become soft and juicy and most definitely pass the smush test.

SPICED OIL

1 tsp ground cumin

1 tsp ground coriander

1 tsp garlic granules or garlic powder

1 tsp onion granules or onion powder

2 tsp (2 g) Italian seasoning

2 tbsp (30 ml) avocado or olive oil

SALMON AND VEGETABLES

12 oz (350 g) baby yellow potatoes, quartered lengthwise

Black pepper, as needed

4 (4-oz [120-g]) skinless salmon fillets, rainbow trout also works

Salt, as needed (optional, for kids 12+ months)

1 small yellow bell pepper, cut into ¼" (6-mm)-thick strips or medium pieces

½ medium zucchini, thickly sliced

½ cup (75 g) cherry or grape tomatoes, halved lengthwise

1 medium lemon, thinly sliced

To make the spiced oil, mix together the cumin, coriander, garlic granules, onion granules, Italian seasoning and oil in a small bowl. Set the spiced oil aside.

To make the salmon and vegetables, preheat the oven to 400°F (200°C, gas mark 6).

Place the potatoes on a large baking sheet. Season them with black pepper and half of the spiced oil. Toss the potatoes until they are well coated. Roast for 25 minutes.

Meanwhile, place the salmon fillets on a plate. Evenly distribute the remaining seasoned oil over the fillets, and season them with black pepper and salt (if using).

Remove the potatoes from the oven and add the bell pepper, zucchini and cherry tomatoes to the baking sheet. Stir the vegetables well, making sure they take on some of the seasoning from the potatoes. Using a spoon, move things around to make space for the salmon fillets. Add the fillets to the baking sheet, making sure they are not overlapping. Place a lemon slice over each fillet.

Roast the salmon and vegetables for 15 to 20 minutes, or until the potatoes and vegetables are fork-tender and the salmon is opaque and flakes easily with a fork. Taste the potatoes and vegetables for seasoning and add additional salt (if using).

Allow the salmon and vegetables to cool sufficiently before serving them to your child. Make sure to remove the lemon slice from your baby's portion. Use a fork to break the salmon into larger chunks for early eaters or into flakes for older babies and toddlers.

Store the salmon and vegetables in an airtight container in the refrigerator for up to 3 days. Reheat the salmon and vegetables, covered, in the oven at 375°F (190°C, gas mark 5) for 10 to 15 minutes, or until they are heated through.

SLOW COOKER *and* INSTANT POT® Meals

A cookbook for busy parents would not be complete without a chapter dedicated to slow cooker and Instant Pot meals. These nifty kitchen gadgets allow you to produce hearty and flavorful meals with minimal effort. There's no better feeling than coming home to the delicious smell of dinner enveloping the house—or realizing that you've run out of time to cook that lengthy stew, only for the Instant Pot to come to the rescue and cook it in minutes! I use both of these gadgets several times a week with consistently amazing results, so if you have been on the fence about purchasing either, I can tell you they are well worth the investment.

In this chapter, you will find a range of meals that will look like you've really put your heart and soul into them, when in reality the most you will have done is a bit of chopping and maybe some sautéing. I've made sure to include a variety of cuisines and meal types so that you can keep things interesting and appeal to your family's differing tastes.

If you don't have a slow cooker or Instant Pot, I have included alternative stove and oven instructions for all of the recipes, so you'll still be able to make them—just be aware that when you are using the stove, these meals may not be as quick or simple, and you may want to factor this in when determining which recipes to try.

Carrot Cake Steel-Cut Oatmeal

Did someone say cake for breakfast? This oatmeal recipe is so decadent that it's hard to believe it's nothing more than a bowl of delicious, nutritious goodness—with the added benefit of a veggie exposure! Steel-cut oats have a lower glycemic index than other varieties and will keep your little one feeling satisfied longer. They do take longer to cook, though, which is where the Instant Pot comes in. Just dump everything in the Instant Pot upon waking and let it do its magic—no need to waste time babysitting the oats at the stove! This method of cooking steel-cut oats can be used with any flavor combination; just stick to the same ratio of oats to liquid as your base and add your desired extras.

OATMEAL

1 cup (110 g) shredded carrots

2 cups (320 g) steel-cut oats

2 cups (480 ml) full-fat milk, nondairy milk or water

3 cups (720 ml) water

1 tsp pure vanilla extract

½ tsp ground cinnamon

¼ tsp ground nutmeg

2 tbsp (20 g) chia seeds

ADD-INS

¼ cup (25 g) unsweetened shredded coconut (optional)

⅓ cup (50 g) raisins or roughly chopped dates (optional)

Pure maple syrup, as needed (optional)

INSTANT POT

Combine the carrots, oats, milk, water, vanilla, cinnamon and nutmeg in the Instant Pot (don't add the chia seeds yet). Add the coconut, raisins and maple syrup (if using). Stir to combine.

Lock the lid on the Instant Pot and set the vent to the sealing position. Press Manual (i.e., high pressure) and set the timer for 5 minutes.

Allow the pressure to release naturally for 10 minutes before manually releasing the remaining pressure. Remove the lid, add the chia seeds and stir to combine the ingredients.

STOVE

Combine the milk and water in a large pot over high heat and bring the liquid to a boil. Add the carrots, oats, vanilla, cinnamon, nutmeg, chia seeds, coconut (if using), raisins (if using) and maple syrup (if using). Stir to combine the ingredients, then reduce the heat to low. Simmer the oatmeal for 25 to 30 minutes, or according to the package's instructions, until the oats are tender. Stir the oatmeal often to prevent the oats from sticking to the bottom of the pot, and add more water or milk as needed.

SERVING AND STORAGE

Allow the oatmeal to cool before serving it to your child—you can speed this up by serving the oatmeal on a lipped plate or by adding cold milk. The oatmeal will continue to thicken as it cools, which will make for easier self-feeding. Preload two or three spoons with the oatmeal for baby to practice with.

Store the oatmeal in an airtight container in the refrigerator for up to 3 days. To freeze it, divide the cooled oatmeal into individual portions and freeze them for up to 3 months. Defrost the oatmeal overnight in the refrigerator and gently reheat it on the stove with a splash of milk or water.

Prep Time:
5 minutes

Cook Time:
25 minutes in the Instant Pot; 25 to 30 minutes on the stove

Yield:
Serves 2 adults + 2 children

30 MINUTES OR LESS

MAKE-AHEAD

FREEZER FRIENDLY

VEGAN OPTION

EGG FREE

NUT FREE

SOURCE OF IRON & FIBER

MES

Prep Time:

10 minutes

Cook Time:

25 minutes in the Instant Pot; 35 to 40 minutes on the stove

Yield:

Serves 3 adults + 3 children

VEGAN

DAIRY FREE

EGG FREE

NUT FREE

SOURCE OF IRON, PROTEIN & FIBER

MESSY MEAL

Minestrone Soup

Minestrone soup is a hearty Italian tomato-based soup bursting with punchy, earthy flavor. Not only is this soup a crowd-pleaser, but it's also one of those chunkier soups that babies and toddlers find easier to eat when self-feeding. I'm not going to pretend that it's any less messy than a smooth soup, but it's far more likely to actually get into your baby's tummy!

2 tbsp (30 ml) avocado or olive oil

1 medium yellow onion, diced

2 medium ribs celery, thinly sliced

1 medium zucchini, sliced into half-moons

2 medium carrots, peeled and thickly sliced

2 tsp (6 g) minced garlic

2 tsp (2 g) Italian seasoning

Black pepper, as needed

4 cups (960 ml) low-sodium vegetable stock

2 (15-oz [400-g]) cans crushed or chopped tomatoes, undrained

1 tbsp (15 g) tomato paste

1 (15-oz [400-g]) can cannellini beans, drained and rinsed

2 cups (200 g) dried fusilli pasta

1 cup (150 g) frozen green beans

2 cups (80 g) roughly chopped kale, stems removed

Salt, as needed (optional, for kids 12+ months)

INSTANT POT

Set the Instant Pot to the Sauté mode and adjust it to More or High. Add the oil. Once the display reads Hot, add the onion, celery, zucchini and carrots and mix thoroughly to combine the vegetables. Cook the vegetables for 2 to 3 minutes, stirring often, until they begin to soften.

Add the garlic, Italian seasoning and black pepper and stir the mixture. Cook the vegetables for 1 minute, until the garlic is fragrant. Add the vegetable stock, tomatoes, tomato paste, cannellini beans, pasta and green beans. Stir to combine the ingredients well. Place the kale on top of the mixture, but do not stir it. It's okay if the kale is above the maximum capacity line of the Instant Pot, as it will cook down very quickly and cause no issues.

Cancel the Sauté mode and lock the lid on the Instant Pot. Set the vent to the sealing position, press Manual or Pressure Cook (i.e., high pressure) and set the timer for 5 minutes. Once the cook time is up, carefully quick-release the pressure, remove the lid and stir the soup well. Taste the soup for seasoning and add salt (if using).

STOVE

Heat a large pot over medium-high heat and add the oil. Once the oil is hot, add the onion, celery and carrots, and mix them together thoroughly. Cook the vegetables for 2 to 3 minutes, stirring often, until they begin to soften. Add the garlic, Italian seasoning and black pepper and stir to combine the ingredients. Cook the mixture for 1 minute, until the garlic is fragrant.

(Continued)

Minestrone Soup (Continued)

Add the vegetable stock, tomatoes, tomato paste and cannellini beans, and mix until the ingredients are well combined. Bring the soup to a boil. Reduce the heat to low, partially cover the pot and simmer the soup for 10 minutes. Add the pasta and zucchini, stir to combine the ingredients and cook the soup, uncovered, for 15 to 20 minutes, stirring often, or until the pasta is cooked. During the final 5 minutes of cooking, add the green beans and kale. Stir the soup well and allow it to simmer until the kale is wilted and the green beans are soft. Taste the soup for seasoning and add salt (if using).

SERVING AND STORAGE

Allow the soup to cool sufficiently before serving it to your child in a bowl. For younger babies, drain some of the liquid into a small cup for them to drink. This way they don't miss out on all of that glorious tomatoey goodness!

Store the soup in an airtight container in the refrigerator for up to 3 days. Reheat it on the stove over medium heat.

Baby-Friendly Chicken Curry

We are somewhat obsessed with curries in our house, so it was important for me to introduce my kids to those warming, aromatic spices right from the beginning of starting solids. The goal with this mellow yet wonderfully fragrant Indian-style curry is to introduce babies to those strong flavors, while at the same time holding back on the heat factor. The good thing about Indian food is that mild most certainly doesn't mean bland, and this curry packs a ton of flavor that small kids can still enjoy.

1 lb (450 g) boneless, skinless chicken thighs, cut into 1½" (4-cm) pieces

2 tsp (6 g) ground coriander

2 tsp (6 g) garam masala, divided

Juice of ½ medium lemon

1 tbsp (15 ml) avocado or olive oil

2 tbsp (30 g) unsalted butter or nondairy butter

1 medium yellow onion, diced

2 tsp (6 g) minced garlic

2 tsp (6 g) ground turmeric

2 cups (480 ml) low-sodium chicken stock

2 tbsp (30 g) tomato paste

Black pepper, as needed

2 tbsp (10 g) ground almonds

⅓ cup (80 ml) heavy cream or full-fat coconut cream (see Cook's Tip)

Salt, as needed (optional, for kids 12+ months)

Grain of choice, for serving

Vegetable of choice, for serving

In a large bowl, combine the chicken, coriander, 1 teaspoon of the garam masala and lemon juice. Mix the ingredients well and set the bowl aside.

SLOW COOKER

Heat a large frying pan over medium-high heat and add the oil. Once the oil is hot, add the seasoned chicken in an even layer and sear it for 2 minutes on both sides. Transfer the seared chicken to the slow cooker.

Reduce the heat to medium and add the butter to the same frying pan. Once the butter has melted, add the onion and garlic and sauté them for 2 minutes, stirring often. Add the turmeric and remaining 1 teaspoon of garam masala. Stir to combine the ingredients and cook the mixture for 1 minute, until the spices are fragrant. Add the chicken stock and stir the mixture again, loosening up any brown bits stuck to the frying pan. Pour this mixture into the slow cooker. Add the tomato paste and black pepper and stir to thoroughly combine the ingredients.

Cover the slow cooker and cook the curry for 3 to 4 hours on high or for 6 to 7 hours on low, until the chicken is tender and the sauce has thickened. During the final 10 minutes of cooking, stir in the almonds and heavy cream.

(Continued)

Prep Time:
15 minutes

Cook Time:
3 to 4 hours on high or 6 to 7 hours on low in the slow cooker; 40 to 45 minutes on the stove

Yield:
Serves 2 adults + 2 children

MAKE-AHEAD

FREEZER FRIENDLY

DAIRY-FREE OPTION

EGG FREE

SOURCE OF IRON & PROTEIN

MESSY MEAL

Baby-Friendly Chicken Curry (Continued)

STOVE

Heat a large frying pan over medium-high heat and add the oil. Once the oil is hot, add the chicken in an even layer and sear it for 2 to 3 minutes on both sides. Reduce the heat to low and add the butter to the frying pan. Stir the butter until it has melted, then add the onion, garlic, turmeric and the remaining 1 teaspoon of garam masala. Stir the ingredients to combine them. Cook the mixture for 2 to 3 minutes, stirring often, until the onion begins to soften.

Add the chicken stock, tomato paste and black pepper. Stir the ingredients well, loosening up any brown bits stuck to the frying pan. Bring the mixture to a boil, reduce the heat to low and cover the frying pan with its lid. Simmer the mixture for 40 to 45 minutes, stirring often to make sure it doesn't stick to the bottom of the frying pan and adding water as needed. During the final 10 minutes of the cook time, stir in the almonds and heavy cream.

SERVING AND STORAGE

Taste the curry for seasoning and add salt (if using).

Serve the curry with the grain of choice and a vegetable on the side (see Nutritionist's Tip).

Store the curry in an airtight container in the refrigerator for up to 3 days. To freeze it, divide the cooled curry into individual portions and freeze them for up to 3 months. Defrost the curry overnight in the refrigerator and reheat it in a saucepan with a splash of water.

COOK'S TIP: If you decide to use coconut cream instead of heavy cream, to store the curry, freeze the individual portions of curry before adding the coconut cream. Add it when you reheat the curry.

NUTRITIONIST'S TIP: If you are serving a grain such as rice to 6 to 12 month olds, try stirring a bit of the curry sauce into the grain to allow the grain to be eaten with a spoon or to be picked up by hand more easily.

Sweet Potato and Three-Bean Chili

The longer chili cooks, the tastier it becomes. But if you're anything like me, you probably don't have the time or the energy to babysit it at the stove to make sure it doesn't dry out or stick to the pan. So naturally, it's the trusty slow cooker to the rescue! Not only does slow-cooking maximize those fragrant flavors, but it also makes the beans so soft that they melt in your mouth, which is ideal for younger babies and toddlers.

Prep Time:
10 minutes

Cook Time:
4 hours on high or 7 to 8 hours on low in the slow cooker; 40 to 45 minutes on the stove

Yield:
Serves 3 adults + 3 children

MAKE-AHEAD

FREEZER FRIENDLY

VEGAN

DAIRY FREE

EGG FREE

NUT FREE

SOURCE OF IRON, PROTEIN & FIBER

MESSY MEAL

CHILI

1 tbsp (15 ml) olive oil

1 medium red onion, diced

1 large red bell pepper, cut into large pieces

2 tsp (6 g) minced garlic

2 tsp (6 g) mild chili powder

2 tsp (6 g) smoked paprika

1 tsp ground cumin

1 tbsp (3 g) dried oregano

2 medium sweet potatoes, peeled and cut into 1½" (4-cm) pieces

1 (15-oz [400-g]) can kidney beans, drained and rinsed

1 (15-oz [400-g]) can cannellini beans, drained and rinsed

1 (15-oz [400-g]) can black beans, drained and rinsed

2 (15-oz [400-g]) cans chopped tomatoes, undrained

1 cup (240 ml) low-sodium vegetable or chicken stock

1 tbsp (15 g) tomato paste

Black pepper, as needed

Salt, as needed (optional, for kids 12+ months)

Basmati rice or other grain of choice, for serving

Vegetable of choice, for serving

GARNISHES

Thickly or thinly sliced avocado, as needed (optional)

Sour cream or full-fat plain Greek yogurt, as needed (optional)

Grated Cheddar cheese, as needed (optional)

Finely chopped fresh cilantro, as needed (optional)

Heat a large frying pan (if using a slow cooker) or pot (if cooking on the stove) over medium heat and add the oil. Once the oil is hot, add the onion and red bell pepper and sauté them for 2 minutes. Add the garlic, chili powder, smoked paprika, cumin and oregano. Stir the ingredients well and cook them for 1 minute, until the garlic is fragrant.

SLOW COOKER

Transfer the mixture to the slow cooker. Add the sweet potatoes, kidney beans, cannellini beans, black beans, tomatoes, vegetable stock, tomato paste and black pepper. Stir the chili well, cover the slow cooker and cook the chili for 4 hours on high or for 7 to 8 hours on low. Stir the chili prior to serving.

STOVE

Add the sweet potatoes, kidney beans, cannellini beans, black beans, tomatoes, vegetable stock, tomato paste and black pepper. Bring the chili to a boil. Reduce the heat to low, cover the pot and simmer the chili for 40 to 45 minutes, stirring often and adding water if needed. If the chili is not thick enough once it is cooked, increase the heat to medium, remove the pot's lid and cook the chili until it reaches your desired consistency.

(Continued)

Sweet Potato and Three-Bean Chili (Continued)

SERVING AND STORAGE

Taste the chili for seasoning and add salt (if using).

Serve the chili in a bowl with the avocado (if using), sour cream (if using), Cheddar cheese (if using) and cilantro (if using), or on a lipped plate with the rice and an additional vegetable of choice.

Store the chili in an airtight container in the refrigerator for up to 3 days. To freeze it, divide the cooled chili into individual portions and freeze them for up to 3 months. Defrost the chili overnight in the refrigerator before reheating it on the stove with a splash of water.

NUTRITIONIST'S TIP: Try mashing the beans before serving them to babies in the 6 to 9 month range. This is especially helpful if you cooked the chili on the stove, as the beans will be firmer than cooking in the slow cooker. Not only does mashing beans make them easier for babies to pick up in their palms, but it also helps them digest the beans more easily. But don't be alarmed if you see some whole beans come out the other end!

Chicken and Barley Casserole

If you've ever shied away from cooking barley because you're not sure how to go about it, then this recipe is a great place to start. Barley is a nutritious, affordable and hearty grain that has a distinctive nutty flavor and slightly chewy texture, which makes it perfect for soups, stews and casseroles.

In this dish, barley does a wonderful job of plumping up and soaking in all of the delicious flavors from the chicken. And I love that it rounds out the meal perfectly so that I don't have to cook a carb on the side!

4 whole chicken legs (drumsticks and thighs), skins removed

1½ tbsp (14 g) poultry seasoning or chicken seasoning, divided

Juice of 1 medium lemon

2 tbsp (30 ml) avocado or olive oil

1 medium leek, thinly sliced

2 medium ribs celery, thinly sliced (see Nutritionist's Tip)

3 medium carrots, thickly sliced

2 tsp (6 g) minced garlic

1 tsp dried rosemary

1 tbsp (8 g) all-purpose flour

2 cups (480 ml) low-sodium chicken stock

1 cup (240 ml) water (for the oven method)

1 cup (200 g) pearl barley

Black pepper, as needed

Salt, as needed (optional, for kids 12+ months)

Vegetable or fruit of choice, for serving (optional)

In a large bowl, combine the chicken legs, 1 tablespoon (9 g) of the poultry seasoning and the lemon juice. Mix until the ingredients are well combined.

INSTANT POT

Set the Instant Pot to the Sauté setting, adjust it to More or High and add the oil. Once the display reads Hot, add the chicken legs in an even layer and sear them for 2 minutes on both sides. Transfer the chicken legs to a plate and set them aside.

Add the leek, celery, carrots, garlic and rosemary to the Instant Pot. Stir to combine the ingredients and cook them for 2 to 3 minutes, stirring often, until they begin to soften. Add the remaining ½ tablespoon (5 g) of poultry seasoning and the flour and mix the ingredients together. Add the chicken stock, barley and black pepper. Stir to combine the ingredients, then add the chicken legs, nestling them into the mixture.

Cancel the Sauté setting and lock the lid on the Instant Pot. Set the vent to the sealing position, press Manual or Pressure Cook (i.e., high pressure) and set the timer for 12 minutes. Once the time is up, let the pressure release naturally for 10 minutes before manually releasing the remaining pressure. Remove the lid and gently stir the casserole.

(Continued)

Prep Time:
10 minutes

Cook Time:
40 to 45 minutes in the Instant Pot; 1 to 1¼ hours in the oven

Yield:
Serves 2 adults + 2 children

MAKE-AHEAD

FREEZER FRIENDLY

DAIRY FREE

EGG FREE

NUT FREE

SOURCE OF IRON, PROTEIN & FIBER

MESSY MEAL

Chicken and Barley Casserole (Continued)

OVEN

Preheat the oven to 375°F (190°C, gas mark 5). Heat a large oven- and stove-safe casserole dish or Dutch oven over medium-high heat and add the oil. Once the oil is hot, add the chicken legs in an even layer and sear them for 2 minutes on both sides. Transfer the chicken legs to a plate and set them aside.

Add the leek, celery, carrots, garlic and rosemary to the casserole dish. Stir the ingredients together and cook them for 2 to 3 minutes, stirring often, until they begin to soften. Add the remaining ½ tablespoon (5 g) of poultry seasoning and the flour and mix the ingredients together. Add the chicken stock, water, barley and black pepper. Stir to combine the ingredients, then add the chicken legs, nestling them into the mixture.

Cover the casserole dish with its lid and bake the casserole for 1 to 1¼ hours, stirring the casserole gently halfway through the cooking time. If needed, carefully place the casserole dish back on the stove and simmer the casserole over medium heat to thicken the liquid to your liking.

SERVING AND STORAGE

Taste the casserole for seasoning and add salt (if using).

Allow the casserole to cool sufficiently before serving it to your child, removing any bone or gristle from the chicken for kids under 4 years old. Serve the chicken in larger, easy-to-hold strips for early eaters, or shred the chicken with a fork for older babies and toddlers. This meal is perfectly balanced, but feel free to add an extra vegetable or some fruit on the side for more variety.

Store the casserole in an airtight container in the refrigerator for up to 3 days. To freeze it, divide the cooled casserole into individual portions and freeze them for up to 3 months. Defrost the casserole overnight in the refrigerator before reheating it in a saucepan with a splash of water.

NUTRITIONIST'S TIP: Raw celery can be a choking hazard for kids younger than 4 years. Cooking it in a recipe like this is a great way to expose your child to it in a safe way.

Prep Time:

5 minutes

Cook Time:

20 minutes in the Instant Pot; 25 to 30 minutes on the stove

Yield:

2 cups (510 g)

30 MINUTES OR LESS

MAKE-AHEAD

FREEZER FRIENDLY

VEGAN

NUT FREE

SOURCE OF FIBER

MESSY MEAL

Big-Flavor Cinnamon Applesauce

I couldn't write a weaning cookbook without including a recipe for one of the most classic baby-friendly foods! Even as an adult, I find myself drawn to the sweet, slightly tart yet savory flavor of applesauce—it never fails to comfort me. While applesauce is typically easy to make, it's even easier when you use the Instant Pot, as all you have to do is cut up a bag of apples and you are pretty much done—no peeling involved! Pressure-cooking means that the skins, along with all their nutritious goodness, will be soft enough to be blended into a silky sauce. Not only that, the flavors intensify in a big way, making the applesauce rich, decadent and truly addictive. If you are making this recipe on the stovetop, be sure to peel the apples, as the skins won't break down as they do in a pressure cooker.

6 medium apples (any variety), peeled (for the stove method), cored and chopped into ¾" (2-cm) pieces

1 to 2 (2" [5-cm]) cinnamon sticks or 1 tsp ground cinnamon, or to taste

¼ cup (60 ml) water for the Instant Pot method or ½ cup (120 ml) for the stove method

INSTANT POT

In the Instant Pot, combine the apples (unpeeled), cinnamon sticks and water. Lock the lid on the Instant Pot and set the vent to the sealing position. Press Manual or Pressure Cook (i.e., high pressure) and set the timer for 4 minutes. When the time is up, let the pressure release naturally for 10 minutes before manually releasing the remaining pressure. Remove the Instant Pot's lid, discard the cinnamon sticks and stir to mix the ingredients together.

STOVE

Combine the apples (peeled), cinnamon sticks and water in a medium pot over medium heat. Mix the ingredients together. Cook the mixture for 3 to 5 minutes, until it is warmed through.

Reduce the heat to low, cover the pot and cook the mixture for 20 to 25 minutes, or until the apples are very soft, stirring halfway through the cooking time. Discard the cinnamon sticks and stir to mix the ingredients together.

SERVING AND STORAGE

Transfer the cooked apple mixture to a large bowl and use an immersion blender to blend the apples until they are smooth and silky. Alternatively, you can use a countertop blender or food processor and blend the apple mixture on medium speed. Take extra care, as the apples will be very hot and may try to fly upward when you begin blending.

Serve the applesauce as part of a meal or snack, or use it as a natural sweetener for yogurt, oatmeal and baked goods.

Store the applesauce in an airtight container in the refrigerator for up to 1 week. To freeze the applesauce, divide it evenly among ice cube trays and freeze it for up to 3 months.

Shredded Beef Brisket

When serving beef to babies, the more tender it is the better. And that's why I love this brisket recipe. Once you've browned the beef, it is cooked low and slow and requires very little attention. This can be done in the slow cooker or in the oven, and the result is incredibly soft and juicy pieces of beef steeped in a lavishly rich sauce—it will melt in your mouth. Another huge plus is that shredded beef can wear many hats. It can be served over mashed potatoes, with cooked grains, in a fajita-style wrap or nestled between burger buns with coleslaw. Leftovers can be used to make tacos, quesadillas, chili, enchiladas or shepherd's pie—just to name a few possibilities. It's the perfect low-effort meal and is truly worth the wait!

DRY RUB

1 tsp onion granules or onion powder

1 tsp garlic granules or garlic powder

1 tsp smoked paprika

1 tsp ground cumin

1 tsp dried oregano

Black pepper, as needed

BRISKET

4 lb (1.8 kg) beef brisket

1 cup (240 ml) low-sodium beef stock

1 (15-oz [400-g]) can chopped tomatoes, undrained, or crushed tomatoes

1 tbsp (15 g) Dijon mustard

1 tbsp (15 g) tomato paste

1 tbsp (15 ml) Worcestershire sauce

2 tbsp (30 ml) avocado or olive oil, plus more if needed

1 large red onion, halved and thinly sliced

2 tsp (6 g) minced garlic

Salt, as needed (optional, for kids 12+ months)

Mashed potatoes, for serving

Vegetables, for serving

To make the dry rub, mix together the onion granules, garlic granules, smoked paprika, cumin, oregano and black pepper in a small bowl.

To begin preparing the brisket, sprinkle the dry rub over both sides of the brisket. Set the brisket aside.

Whisk together the beef stock, tomatoes, mustard, tomato paste and Worcestershire sauce in a medium bowl. Set the mixture aside.

SLOW COOKER

Heat a very large frying pan over high heat and add the oil. Once the oil is hot, carefully place the brisket into the frying pan and sear it for 3 to 4 minutes on both sides. Transfer the brisket to the slow cooker.

Reduce the heat to medium and add a little more oil to the frying pan, if needed. Add the onion and garlic and cook them for 2 to 3 minutes, stirring often.

Add the stock and tomato mixture and mix until everything is well combined. Bring the mixture to a boil, using a wooden spoon to loosen any brown bits stuck to the frying pan.

Pour the mixture into the slow cooker. Cover the slow cooker and cook the brisket for 4 to 5 hours on high or 8 to 9 hours on low, or until the brisket is tender and falls apart.

(Continued)

Prep Time:
15 to 20 minutes

Cook Time:
4 to 5 hours on high or 8 to 9 hours on low in the slow cooker; 3½ to 4 hours in the oven

Yield:
Serves 4 adults + 4 children

MAKE-AHEAD

FREEZER FRIENDLY

NUT FREE

SOURCE OF IRON & PROTEIN

OVEN

Preheat the oven to 350°F (180°C, gas mark 4). Heat a large oven- and stove-safe casserole dish or Dutch oven over high heat and add the oil. Once the oil is hot, carefully place the brisket into the casserole dish and sear it for 4 to 5 minutes on both sides. Remove the brisket and set it aside.

Reduce the heat to medium and add a little more oil if needed. Add the onion and garlic and cook them for 2 to 3 minutes, stirring often.

Add the stock and tomato mixture and mix until everything is well combined. Bring the mixture to a boil, using a wooden spoon to loosen any brown bits stuck to the casserole dish. Turn off the heat, add the brisket to the casserole dish and spoon some of the sauce over the top.

Cover the casserole dish and roast the brisket for 3½ to 4 hours, or until the beef is tender and falling apart. Check on the beef halfway through the cook time and add some water if needed.

SERVING AND STORAGE

Gently place the cooked brisket on a large cutting board and use two forks to shred the beef, then transfer it to a serving dish. Whisk the leftover pan juices until they are well combined and spoon a small amount over the shredded beef to keep it moist, but not so much that it becomes soupy. Taste the beef for seasoning and add salt (if using). Serve the beef with the mashed potatoes and vegetables of choice, or refer to the recipe headnote for more serving ideas.

Store the shredded brisket in an airtight container in the refrigerator for up to 3 days, or freeze it in a freezer-safe container for up to 3 months. Defrost the brisket overnight in the refrigerator before reheating it in a saucepan on the stove with a splash of water.

Chicken, Mushroom and Pea Risotto

Risotto is one of those classic, comforting meals that is always a hit with my kids, but one major downside is that the traditional method of cooking risotto requires a lot of stove babysitting, with constant stirring and adding broth—not the best combination for a hectic evening!

I soon discovered that cooking risotto in the Instant Pot is a simple and low-effort alternative that still produces the same deliciously creamy, authentic results. Just sauté the chicken and vegetables and let the Instant Pot do the rest! You can also bake this risotto, which is still much easier than using a stove, but you'll have to check on it halfway through to give it a stir.

1 lb (450 g) diced boneless, skinless chicken breasts

1 tsp onion granules or onion powder

Black pepper, as needed

1 tbsp (15 ml) avocado or olive oil

2 tbsp (30 g) unsalted butter

1 cup (70 g) thickly sliced white button or chestnut mushrooms

1 small leek, thinly sliced

2 tsp (6 g) minced garlic

2 tsp (2 g) Italian seasoning

2 cups (400 g) arborio (risotto) rice

4 cups (960 ml) low-sodium chicken stock for the Instant Pot method or 3 cups (720 ml) for the oven method

1 cup (135 g) frozen peas

⅓ cup (35 g) grated Parmesan cheese

Salt, as needed (optional, for kids 12+ months)

In a medium bowl, combine the chicken, onion granules and black pepper. Stir the chicken to coat it in the spices.

INSTANT POT

Set the Instant Pot to the Sauté setting and adjust it to More or High and add the oil. Once the display reads Hot, add the chicken in an even layer and sear it for 2 minutes on both sides. Transfer the chicken to a plate and set it aside.

Add the butter to the Instant Pot. Once it has melted, add the mushrooms and sauté them for 2 minutes. Add the leek, garlic and Italian seasoning. Cook the mixture for 2 minutes, stirring often, until the vegetables are soft and fragrant.

Add the chicken back to the Instant Pot, then add the rice, chicken stock and peas. Stir to combine the ingredients. Cancel the Sauté setting and lock the lid on the Instant Pot. Set the vent to the sealing position, press Manual or Pressure Cook (i.e., high pressure) and set the timer for 5 minutes. Once the time is up, carefully release the pressure manually and remove the lid.

OVEN

Preheat the oven to 400°F (200°C, gas mark 6). Heat a large oven- and stove-safe casserole dish over medium-high heat and add the oil. Once the oil is hot, add the chicken and sear it for 2 minutes on both sides. Transfer the chicken to a plate and set it aside.

Add the butter to the casserole dish. Once it has melted, add the mushrooms and sauté them for 2 minutes. Add the leek, garlic and Italian seasoning. Cook the mixture for 2 minutes, stirring often, until the vegetables are soft and fragrant.

(Continued)

Prep Time:
10 to 12 minutes

Cook Time:
20 minutes in the Instant Pot; 25 to 30 minutes in the oven

Yield:
Serves 2 adults + 3 children

EGG FREE

NUT FREE

SOURCE OF IRON & PROTEIN

MESSY MEAL

Chicken, Mushroom and Pea Risotto (Continued)

Add the chicken back to the casserole dish, then add the rice, chicken stock and peas. Stir to combine the ingredients.

Bring the mixture to a boil and turn off the heat. Cover the casserole dish with a lid and bake the risotto for 20 to 25 minutes, stirring it once halfway through the cooking time, or until the rice is fully cooked.

SERVING AND STORAGE

Stir the Parmesan cheese into the hot risotto. Season the risotto with additional black pepper, if desired. Taste the risotto for seasoning and add salt (if using).

Allow the risotto to cool sufficiently before serving it to your child. Whole cooked peas are safe to serve, but you may prefer to mash them with a fork for younger babies. Preload the risotto onto a spoon or try rolling the cooled risotto into balls for easy self-feeding.

Store the risotto in an airtight container in the refrigerator for up to 3 days. Reheat it in a saucepan on the stove with a splash of water.

Lentil Bolognese

I love a good Bolognese—it's simple to make, family friendly and it freezes fabulously well for quick and easy meals in a pinch. Bolognese can be just as hearty and flavorful when made with lentils as it is with meat, especially when it's cooked in the slow cooker. If you're looking for an alternative, lighter version of traditional meat-based Bolognese that doesn't compromise on nutrition or those gorgeously pungent and deep Italian flavors, then be sure to give this a go!

1 tbsp (15 ml) avocado or olive oil

1 medium yellow onion, diced

1 medium red bell pepper, diced

1½ cups (100 g) thinly sliced or diced white button or chestnut mushrooms

2 large or 3 medium carrots, grated

2 tsp (6 g) minced garlic

2 tsp (2 g) Italian seasoning or dried mixed herbs

8 oz (230 g) brown lentils, rinsed and picked through

1 cup (240 ml) low-sodium vegetable stock

1 (15-oz [400-g]) can crushed or chopped tomatoes, undrained

28 oz (800 g) passata or strained tomatoes

1 tbsp (15 ml) regular or vegan Worcestershire sauce

Black pepper, as needed

Salt, as needed (optional, for kids 12+ months)

Cooked pasta of choice (such as fusilli, rigatoni or spaghetti), rice or baked potatoes, for serving

Vegetables of choice, for serving

Heat a large frying pan if using the slow cooker method or a large pot if using the stove method over medium-high heat and add the oil. Once the oil is hot, add the onion, bell pepper, mushrooms and carrots and mix the vegetables well. Sauté them for 4 to 5 minutes, then add the garlic and Italian seasoning. Mix the ingredients well and cook them for 1 minute, until the garlic and herbs are fragrant.

SLOW COOKER

Transfer the sautéed mixture to the slow cooker. Add the lentils, vegetable stock, crushed tomatoes, passata, Worcestershire sauce and black pepper. Stir the mixture well, cover the slow cooker and cook the Bolognese for 4 to 5 hours on high or for 8 to 9 hours on low.

STOVE

Add the lentils, vegetable stock, crushed tomatoes, passata, Worcestershire sauce and black pepper to the pot. Stir to combine the ingredients. Bring the mixture to a boil, reduce the heat to low, cover the pot and simmer the Bolognese for 55 to 60 minutes, or until the lentils are tender. Stir often to prevent it from sticking to the pot. If the liquid starts to reduce too much, add water as needed.

Turn off the heat and let the Bolognese rest for at least 10 minutes before serving. This will help the flavors mingle more.

SERVING AND STORAGE

Taste the Bolognese for seasoning and add salt (if using). Serve the sauce mixed with the pasta of choice with an additional vegetable on the side. Alternatively, serve the sauce mixed through rice or on a baked potato.

Store the Bolognese in an airtight container in the refrigerator for up to 3 days. To freeze it, divide the Bolognese into individual portions and freeze them for up to 3 months. Defrost before reheating on the stove with a splash of water.

Prep Time:
10 minutes

Cook Time:
4 to 5 hours on high or 8 to 9 hours on low in the slow cooker; 55 to 60 minutes on the stove

Yield:
Serves 3 adults + 3 children

MAKE-AHEAD

FREEZER FRIENDLY

VEGAN OPTION

DAIRY FREE

NUT FREE

SOURCE OF IRON, PROTEIN & FIBER

MESSY MEAL

Prep Time:
15 MINUTES

Cook Time:
4 to 5 hours on high or 8 to 9 hours on low in the slow cooker; 2 to 2½ hours in the oven

Yield:
Serves 6 to 8

MAKE-AHEAD

FREEZER FRIENDLY

DAIRY FREE

EGG FREE

NUT FREE

SOURCE OF IRON & PROTEIN

MESSY MEAL

Moroccan Lamb Stew

If you want to come home to the most enchanting aroma coming from your kitchen, then this slow-cooked Moroccan dish is a must! Take your family's taste buds on a trip to North Africa with an explosion of warm aromatic spices coupled with mild notes of sweet apricot, all of which are infused into juicy, tender chunks of lamb. Every time I serve this dish to my family, I hear nothing but the sounds of cutlery clinking on plates. You know you have hit the dinnertime jackpot when everyone is too focused on enjoying the flavors to notice anything else!

Besides slow-cooking, there are many ways to cook this stew. A more traditional approach would be to cook it in the oven, and I have included the instructions for that method here. Oven-cooking is great if you plan to be at home and will have your hands free to check on this dish occasionally.

SPICE BLEND

2 tsp (6 g) smoked paprika

2 tsp (6 g) ground turmeric

2 tsp (6 g) ground cinnamon

1 tsp ground coriander

1 tsp dried thyme

STEW

2½ lb (1.1 kg) cubed lamb shoulder (I recommend 2½" [6-cm] cubes)

1 tbsp (15 ml) avocado or olive oil

1 large red onion, halved and thinly sliced

1 tbsp (9 g) minced garlic

2 cups (480 ml) low-sodium beef stock

½ cup (80 g) dried apricots, roughly chopped

2 medium carrots, thickly sliced

2 large yellow potatoes, peeled and cut into large pieces

2 (15-oz [400-g]) cans chopped tomatoes, undrained

STEW (CONTINUED)

Black pepper, as needed

Salt, as needed (optional, for kids 12+ months)

Mashed potatoes, for serving

Steamed or roasted broccoli, for serving

To make the spice blend, combine the smoked paprika, turmeric, cinnamon, coriander and thyme in a small bowl.

To begin preparing the stew, place the lamb in a large bowl. Sprinkle half of the spice blend over the lamb and mix until all of the lamb pieces are coated in the spices.

SLOW COOKER

Heat a large frying pan over medium-high heat and add the oil. Once the oil is hot, add the lamb pieces in an even layer and sear them for 2 minutes on both sides. You may need to do this in batches. Transfer the cooked lamb to the slow cooker.

Add the onion, garlic and the remaining half of the spice blend to the frying pan, and mix the ingredients together. Cook the mixture for 2 minutes, stirring often. Add the beef stock and bring the mixture to a boil, using a wooden spoon to loosen any brown bits stuck to the frying pan. Pour the mixture into the slow cooker.

Add the apricots, carrots, potatoes, tomatoes and black pepper to the slow cooker. Stir to combine the ingredients. Cover the slow cooker and cook the stew for 4 to 5 hours on high or for 8 to 9 hours on low.

(Continued)

Moroccan Lamb Stew (Continued)

OVEN

Preheat the oven to 350°F (180°C, gas mark 4). Heat a large oven- and stove-safe casserole dish or Dutch oven over medium-high heat and add the oil. Once the oil is hot, add the lamb pieces in an even layer and sear them for 2 minutes on both sides. You may need to do this in batches.

Add the onion, garlic and the remaining half of the spice blend and mix the ingredients together. Cook the mixture for 2 minutes, stirring often. Add the beef stock and bring the mixture to a boil, using a wooden spoon to loosen any brown bits stuck to the casserole dish. Add the apricots, carrots, potatoes, tomatoes and black pepper. Mix the ingredients well, cover the casserole dish and transfer it to the oven. Cook the stew for 2 to 2½ hours, stirring it once halfway through the cooking time, or until the lamb is soft and the vegetables are fork-tender.

SERVING AND STORAGE

Taste the stew for seasoning and add salt (if using). Serve the stew with the mashed potatoes and some steamed broccoli on the side. The chunks of lamb will be tender and will melt in the mouth, but you may prefer to cut it up into bite-sized pieces or shred it for babies who are working on their pincer grasp.

Store the stew in an airtight container in the refrigerator for up to 3 days. To freeze the stew, place it in a freezer-safe container and freeze it for up to 3 months. Defrost the stew in the refrigerator before reheating it in a saucepan on the stove with a splash of water.

GOOD TO KNOW: This recipe makes quite a lot of stew and is perfect for large families or for entertaining. You may wish to halve the recipe if you have a smaller family or a small slow cooker.

Bonus Time-Saving Tips

As busy parents, we often feel like we are racing against the clock. We're almost always trying to find ways to get through our day-to-day commitments as fast as we possibly can! And while this is most definitely an important skill to acquire when you have small kids and a hectic schedule, it's not always possible to achieve in every situation, or even long term. What's more, in a lot of cases it can lead to exhaustion, which in turn runs the risk of an eventual mommy or daddy meltdown—I can personally attest, as I've had my fair share!

What I have learned through my experiences is that time is managed far more effectively if we use it to work smarter instead of harder. Working smarter means that we free up and utilize pockets of time over the course of the week or month, instead of trying to cram everything into small windows day to day. In this chapter, I will talk you through some of the ways you can work smarter, and how it can help you preserve your sanity as you navigate the journey of baby-led weaning and feeding your family.

Meal Planning

Meal planning is my number one strategy for staying organized, reducing stress and making healthy, varied home-cooked meals a reality!

For some of you, meal planning might seem like a rigid concept that doesn't leave space for flexibility, but that doesn't have to be the case. To make meal planning flexible, I recommend planning meals as "options" instead of allocating them to specific days. This makes following a meal plan far less rigid and means that if you don't fancy a chicken casserole on Sunday, you can switch it out for another option.

There are several other benefits to meal planning:

✓ **SAVED TIME.** No more wasted time wondering what to cook at mealtimes and frantically rummaging through the refrigerator, trying to piece together a meal with your baby attached to your hip. Not to mention the time spent on extra trips to the grocery store to pick up what you need. When you have a meal plan, you know exactly where you are and what you need to do. Meal planning also allows you to get everything you need in a single shopping trip so you have everything on hand.

✓ **MORE VARIETY.** Meal planning encourages variety, surprisingly enough, which is especially useful during those first few months of weaning, when there is a particular focus on introducing a wide variety of foods to your baby. When you plan your meals ahead of time, you are much less likely to repeat meals over and over. Seeing your meals written down allows you to get a clear picture of your food week and makes it much easier to incorporate more variety into your meals over the course of the weeks and months.

✓ **SAVED MONEY.** Having a meal plan will transform the way you shop. You are far more aware of what you do and do not need, and this awareness helps reduce impulse buying. Additionally, you are much less likely to order takeout when you have a meal plan in place—which is just as well, as many takeout options are high in sodium and not suitable for babies under a year old. Having everything ready to go means you are more likely to follow through with cooking.

Online Grocery Shopping

Online grocery shopping has come a long way over the years—and as a busy mom of four, I'd be truly lost without it! The days of grocery shopping alone and having some "me time" are few and far between, so I have adapted my approach to fit my hectic schedule. Life is much easier as a result.

A lot of stores now offer the option of "click and collect" grocery shopping, where you can order online and collect your groceries curbside at the store, without even having to leave your vehicle. You can pick up your groceries on your way home without having to bundle your baby in and out of the car!

Here are a few more perks of shopping for groceries online:

✓ **SAVED TIME.** If you are looking for ways to spend more quality time with your baby or free up an hour for that baby class you've been wanting to sign up for, online grocery shopping is a great place to start. You will save precious time by not having to hunt through the store for what you need and wait at the checkout. Even better, you'll avoid the most infuriating situation—realizing you have forgotten something when you are already home and having to go back to the store! With online shopping, you can double-check your cart for missed or forgotten items right up until the night before pickup or delivery.

✓ **CONVENIENCE.** Avoid crowds, browse the virtual aisles in your own time and let someone else gather your items. In some cases, stores will even deliver the items to your home. It's a massive game changer if you would otherwise have to shop with your baby or toddler, because let's be honest—for most of us, grocery shopping with kids is not an easy task!

✓ **SAVED MONEY.** It can be hard to fully concentrate when shopping with a baby or toddler, and a lack of focus can make it especially difficult to take the time you need to compare prices and seek out the best deals available. Shopping for groceries online allows you to keep track of what you are spending as you go. You are less likely to buy impulsively and go over your budget—especially if you have a meal plan—when you can see the balance in real time. You will find it much easier to compare prices so that you can get the best deals possible.

Batch-Cooking and Freezing

I talk about my love for making meals and snacks ahead of time in chapter 2. In this section, I want to provide some practical tips on how to execute this strategy in a realistic way. How you decide to go about batch-cooking will vary depending on your day-to-day circumstances and time constraints, so it's likely you'll need to change your approach as and when needed. Following are a few of my favorite tips:

✓ **COOK ONCE, EAT TWICE.** Repurposing meals is a great way to save time and money and reduce food waste. Leftover cooked chicken can be made into chicken pot pie or chicken noodle soup the next day. And I just love all the different ways you can serve chili: one day with rice, and the next on a baked potato with cheese or in a quesadilla. There are so many ways you can repurpose a meal to save time and make it stretch further.

✓ **BATCH-COOK AS YOU GO.** This is the simplest approach and a great way to build up your freezer stash over time. Work it into your meal plan by doubling up the quantities on recipes you have already planned to cook and freezing the leftovers. You don't always have to freeze your leftovers either—you can use them for lunches throughout the week and keep them varied by switching up the sides. This is another reason why I recommend starting with small portions of food when feeding your baby: They'll likely need less food than you think, and you can refrigerate or freeze leftovers for another day.

✓ **DEVOTE AN AFTERNOON OR TWO.** You'd be surprised how many meals and snacks you can whip up in an afternoon. I find this method is easier to execute when your baby is taking their longest nap of the day or you have a helper available to keep them occupied when they are awake. This is also a great opportunity to get toddlers involved and helping in the kitchen if that's something you enjoy. This method is best if you want to build up your freezer stash more quickly.

Here are some tips for effectively freezing batch-cooked foods:

✓ Freeze meals in individual portions to reduce food waste and defrosting times.

✓ Be sure to label and date portions before freezing. Some meals can look very similar when frozen.

✓ For items that have the potential to stick together, flash-freeze them or separate them with parchment paper before storing them in freezer bags. I have learned this the hard way by having to defrost way more food than I need because the items were stuck together and impossible to separate while frozen.

✓ Freeze food as soon as it has cooled for optimal freshness.

✓ Invest in a variety of freezer-friendly lidded containers and reusable freezing bags. They may seem like an expensive investment initially, but they more than pay for themselves after a few weeks.

Prepping Meals and Snacks

Prepping particular parts of your baby's and family's meals and snacks in advance is another easy way to save time. Food prepped in this way is not necessarily frozen but kept on hand in the refrigerator for easy access.

I recommend these tips for prepping meals and snacks:

✓ As much as possible, prepare parts of a meal in advance, even if it's just a little here and there. Season the meat or prepare the veggies you'll need for dinner. Plan and prep what you'll serve for a snack in an hour or two. Whether it's waking up a little early, utilizing nap times or quiet times or even sneaking in a few minutes while your kids are calm and distracted or the baby is content in a rocker, taking those few minutes to prep can make a big difference during the most challenging parts of the day.

✓ Wash, dry and chop a bunch of fruits and vegetables every few days to have on hand for quick access at snack times and when cooking. Be sure to store them in airtight containers, so that they maintain optimal freshness.

✓ Precooked grains can be safely stored in the refrigerator for up to 4 days, or they can be frozen for up to a month. If you can, cook your grains in advance and reheat them when needed.

✓ For sauces and dressings that store well, make them in advance and keep them in the fridge or freezer for quick and easy additions to meals.

Frozen Prepared Foods

Frozen and prepared foods can be a massively convenient and healthy option for busy families. There are many suitable options for your baby or toddler. We are lucky that in today's food climate we have almost limitless choices and many of them are affordable, nutritious and—most important—delicious! In the sections that follow, I have broken down the categories of shortcut foods that can save your time and sanity without compromising on your goal of serving your family balanced, nutrient-dense foods.

FROZEN FRUITS AND VEGETABLES

When it comes to fruits and vegetables, unless you are picking them yourself, it's generally the case that the frozen variety retain more vitamins and minerals than the fresh. This is because they are picked at the peak of ripeness and frozen shortly afterward. Fresh fruits and vegetables are often picked before they are fully ripe to allow them to survive the journey—often from one country to another—to their destination for sale. This means that they'll likely lose some of their vitamin and mineral content along the way.

This isn't to say that fresh fruits and veggies are substandard and should be avoided. Absolutely not! There are other factors that play a part here too, such as texture and flavor, both of which can change when fresh produce is frozen. But rest assured that you can include frozen fruits and vegetables in your family's diet without compromising on nutrition. Just be sure to always opt for products in which fruits and/or vegetables are the only ingredients.

Here are some benefits of frozen fruits and vegetables:

- ✓ They can retain more vitamins and minerals.
- ✓ They are generally more affordable.
- ✓ They are prewashed and prepared—no peeling and chopping!
- ✓ They often cook faster.
- ✓ They are perfect for adding to smoothies, oatmeal and soups.
- ✓ Shoppers are offered lots of choices for different fruit and vegetable medleys, which are all kept in one easy-to-access place.

PREPARED AND PROCESSED FOODS

Some prepared and processed foods are great for cutting corners and adding quick and easy sides to a meal or snack. Feeding babies and toddlers can feel relentless at times, and you do not have to put yourself through the process of making your own naan breads or whipping up fresh salsa from scratch if you are strapped for time or too tired. Serving some premade, store-bought options can be absolutely fine, and there is no shame in it!

With that said, it is important to be aware that not all processed and premade foods are equal. When feeding babies and toddlers, the main thing to look out for is the sodium content. You may be surprised to learn how much salt lurks in some processed foods, so it is important that you check food labels and ensure you choose low-sodium options. I often find that the generic store-bought brands have less sodium than high-end brands, so don't fall into the trap of thinking the more expensive item is healthier and less salty, as this is often not the case!

You will also want to be mindful of added sugars, as in some cases the sugar content can be pretty high. How sugar is listed on ingredient lists can be misleading too, as food companies often list sugar by various names. Some of these can include buttered syrup, cane juice, dextrose, fructose, maltose, rice syrup and sucrose.

All in all, I recommend shopping around and familiarizing yourself with low-salt and low-sugar options and opting for products with short and simple ingredient lists, as this often makes for a more wholesome product (although not always, so it's important to read labels fully). You won't have to do this for every shopping trip, as you'll soon become familiar with your family's favorites—shopping for healthy foods will become second nature.

PRE-CHOPPED AND PRE-GRATED FOODS

Peeling and chopping vegetables is probably one of the most annoying and time-consuming aspects of cooking and one that can be very difficult to do when you are caring for a young child. But whether we like it or not, we have to do it at least some of the time. If you find it difficult, or don't have the time or energy to pre-chop everything yourself, there are many store-bought options to consider, such as minced garlic and chopped onions, bell peppers, celery and carrots—which always come in handy, as they are bases for many meals, particularly stews and soups. Most frozen fruits and vegetables are pre-chopped and are the most time-saving and efficient way to add variety to a meal. When choosing what to buy, it's best to stick with the frozen variety to minimize nutrient loss and food waste.

Pre-grated cheeses can also be convenient; just be sure to double-check labels for salt content, as pre-grated cheeses can sometimes be higher in salt. Oh, and if you have a food processor, be sure to make good use of the shredder attachment, as this makes chopping and grating a breeze!

HEMP, CHIA AND FLAX SEEDS

My favorite prepared foods for a convenient and instant nutrition boost for babies and toddlers—everyone, really!—are hemp seeds, chia seeds and milled flax seeds. Between them, they contain a variety of essential nutrients, including iron, zinc, omega-3s, calcium and fiber, and they are an incredibly quick, easy and efficient way to significantly ramp up the nutrition in meals and snacks. They're perfect for stirring through oatmeal, adding to smoothies and sprinkling on yogurt, applesauce or toast with nut butter. They can also be used when baking to add extra nutrients to muffins and breads. They have many uses!

These seeds may appear to be expensive at face value, but a little goes a long way! To put it into perspective, a 17-ounce (500-g) bag of any of these seeds lasts me 2 to 3 months, and I have a large family. If you'd prefer not to buy all three varieties, I'd recommend chia seeds as a first choice, as they are the most nutrient-dense and include an impressive five of the essential nutrients that babies and toddlers need to develop and grow.

It's worth noting here that lightly sprinkling chia seeds on foods is not a choking hazard; however, serving very thick chia pudding in a bowl or on a spoon may pose a choking risk, as it can glob up, making it hard to swallow. Be sure to thin out the consistency before serving it.

Feeding Toddlers and Handling Picky Eaters

Once your baby becomes a toddler, you may notice that their eating habits begin to change. What can be most surprising is that your toddler may eat less than they did as a baby. This change can be attributed to many things but is usually a result of significantly slowed growth compared to the growth that occurred in your child's first year. For a lot of toddlers, developmental changes that occur around this age can mean that they may also become picky. A newfound independence, along with the realization that they can make their own choices, is often asserted by pushing the boundaries during mealtimes—especially as their individual tastes and preferences develop. Suddenly your baby who ate everything in sight may no longer eat their once loved-foods, or they may demand specific types of foods or refuse to try anything new or different.

As frustrating as this pickiness is, it is all completely normal, age appropriate and generally nothing to worry about! What's more, we can help our toddlers work through this phase by adjusting the way that we react to this behavior and creating a stress-free environment around mealtimes.

How to Tackle Picky Eating

When looking at ways to address picky eating, it is helpful to think about how we are shaping our child's long-term relationship with food, as opposed to focusing on the short-term victories meal to meal. We often have expectations of what and how much our kids should or should not be eating, and it can feel worrying when they seemingly aren't eating much or when they refuse to eat nutritious foods.

In response, we may be tempted to encourage them to try "just one bite," or to use dessert or other treats as an incentive for them to clean their plates. And while this approach comes from a good place (most of us have been there), enforcing these types of mealtime pressures often backfires in the long term and leads to more picky eating and mealtime struggles. Instead, what is more helpful is to give kids the space and the freedom to eat intuitively and listen to their internal cues regarding food intake.

The Division of Responsibility

Developed by feeding expert Ellyn Satter, the Division of Responsibility (DoR) is a feeding approach that nurtures intuitive eating and helps navigate picky eating phases by providing a nonpressured environment for kids to explore both new and familiar foods.

Research has found that what is most effective when tackling picky eating is to allow kids to eat intuitively and have complete control over their food intake. This doesn't mean that you should only serve the foods that your child likes—instead, give them the freedom to choose what and how much to eat from the meals and snacks that you decide to serve.

Toddlers are very skilled at knowing what their bodies need and when, and this skill is something that comes naturally to them. Often, this translates to them eating only one-fourth of the meal you have served, or refusing to try a new food, or not eating all (or any) of the vegetables on their plate. It can be difficult to accept in the moment, but barring any relevant medical issues, it is okay!

HOW DOES DoR WORK?

The strategy works by outlining the specific roles for both you and your child at mealtimes, and it advises you both to act only within those boundaries.

Those roles are as follows:

- ✓ The parent is responsible for what foods to offer, and when and where to offer them.

- ✓ The child is responsible for whether to eat and how much to eat from the foods offered.

WHY IS DoR IMPORTANT?

Babies are born with an innate hunger gauge that tells them when they are hungry and when they are full. If we consistently encourage them to eat more or less than they need, we override this natural ability. DoR respects this natural ability to self-regulate food intake and encourages children to continue to listen to what their bodies are telling them. DoR not only helps address real-time issues—such as tantrums at the table—but also focuses on long-term results, one of which is to set the foundations for lifelong intuitive eating.

HOW TO IMPLEMENT DoR

Stick to a consistent feeding schedule. Toddlers' tummies can only hold so much food, therefore they need access to food regularly. Creating an eating schedule that offers meals and snacks at regular intervals means that both you and your child can relax in the knowledge that there will be several opportunities to eat throughout the day.

EXAMPLE TODDLER FEEDING SCHEDULE		
MORNING	**AFTERNOON**	**EVENING**
7:00 to 7:30 Breakfast	12:00 to 12:30 Lunch	6:00 to 6:30 Dinner
9:30 to 10:00 Snack	3:00 to 3:30 Snack	Bedtime Snack (optional)*

Some kids will need a bedtime snack, while others will be fine without. Just be sure that if you're offering a bedtime snack or a drink of milk that you clean your toddler's teeth before they go to sleep.

Eating schedules may vary based on your toddler's age and individual needs, but a great place to start is shown in the table above. Keep in mind that the suggested time ranges are just an example and should be adapted to fit with your toddler's routine and/or your family's life. And remember, there will be times when you may stray from your schedule, and that is okay—it's all about consistency, not perfection!

Do not offer food and drinks, apart from water, outside of set mealtimes and snack times. This is often hard to stick to, but it is crucial. We want toddlers to build up an appetite between meals, which in turn will make it more likely that they appreciate the food you're offering them. Allowing toddlers to graze all day undermines mealtimes and snack times and can increase picky eating. If your toddler asks for more food outside of their allocated meals and snacks, explain in an age-appropriate way that there will soon be another opportunity to eat, offer them some water and distract them in the meantime.

Stick to your role. Mealtimes can be hard and food refusal can be worrying, but try your best to stick to your role of serving nutritious meals of your choice, in a time and place of your choosing. There may be times when this just isn't possible, and that's okay. We are looking at the big picture here. Again, it's all about consistency, not perfection!

Always include a "safe" food with meals and snacks. Including one food that you know your toddler will reliably eat with every meal and snack ensures there will always be something your toddler will eat. This further helps reduce the pressure when you are exposing them to a new food and foods they are still learning to like.

Allow your toddler to have as many servings of an individual food as they want. Your toddler may request several servings of one specific food you have served. This is okay so long as there is enough of the food to go around and it won't cause any discomfort, such as an upset tummy. Limiting foods for reasons other than this will only serve to give them power and make them all the more appealing—and ultimately distracting. Leveling the playing field and making all served foods equal allows your toddler to explore foods instinctively and without pressure.

Look at your child's diet over the course of a week or month instead of individual meals. It can be very frustrating to make nutritious meals that go uneaten, but nobody eats perfectly all the time and our tastes and needs fluctuate constantly. Try not to focus on individual meals to determine your child's health; instead, focus on their intake over the course of a week, or even a month, as an indicator of their overall diet. You may be surprised to learn your toddler is adequately filling their nutritional gaps in their own way, at their own pace.

American-British Ingredient Translations

AMERICAN	BRITISH
Heavy cream	Double cream
Scallions (or green onions)	Spring onions
All-purpose flour	Plain flour
Whole wheat flour	Wholemeal flour
Zucchini	Courgette
Ground meat	Minced meat
Grape tomatoes	Plum tomatoes
Snow peas	Mangetout
Broiler	Grill

Resources

For more advice on feeding babies and toddlers, find Simone Ward at:

- ✓ www.zaynesplate.com
- ✓ www.instagram.com/zaynesplate

The Scientific Advisory Committee on Nutrition report on feeding in the first year of life can be accessed at:

- ✓ www.gov.uk/government/publications/feeding-in-the-first-year-of-life-sacn-report

To learn more about Ellyn Satter's Division of Responsibility, visit:

- ✓ https://www.ellynsatterinstitute.org

Renae D'Andrea, MS, RDN, can be found at:

- ✓ newwaysnutrition.com

Recipe Labels Index

	PAGE NUMBER	30 MINUTES OR LESS	MAKE-AHEAD	FREEZER FRIENDLY	LUNCHBOX FRIENDLY	VEGAN/ VEGETARIAN
Spiced Carrot and Lentil Fritters	29		x	x	x	x
Peanut Butter Banana Bread	30		x	x	x	x
Sweet Potato and Broccoli Tots	33		x	x	x	x
Vanilla Oat Waffles	35	x	x	x	x	x
Salmon and Pea Egg Muffins	39		x	x	x	
Savory Snack Bars	40		x	x	x	x
Tuna and Chickpea Fritters	43		x	x	x	
Mixed Berry Muffins	44	x	x	x	x	x
Crispy Coconut Chicken Tenders	47	x	x	x		
Sausage and Herb Pinwheels	49		x	x	x	
Tropical Frozen Yogurt Bark	53		x	x		x
Spinach and Banana French Toast Sticks	54	x	x	x		
Cheese and Tomato Muffins	57		x	x	x	x
Green Smoothie Popsicles	58		x	x		x
Savory Veggie Pancakes	61	x	x	x	x	x
Lemon and Raspberry Oat Cups	62	x	x	x		x
Coconut Chia Pudding	65		x	x		x
Veggie-Loaded Quiche	66		x	x	x	x
Peanut Butter and Jam Overnight Oats	69		x	x		x
Herby Hummus Dip	70	x	x	x		x
Mixed Bean Burgers	73		x	x	x	x
Creamy Tomato and Carrot Pasta with Steam-Roasted Broccolini	77	x				x
Quick Chicken and Gravy	78	x	x	x		
Cheats Veggie Pizza	81	x				x
Spinach and Almond Pesto Pasta	82	x	x	x		x

DAIRY FREE	EGG FREE	NUT FREE	SOURCE OF IRON	SOURCE OF PROTEIN	SOURCE OF FIBER	MESSY MEAL
X		X	X	X	X	
X			X	X		
	X	X			X	
		X	X		X	
		X	X	X		
		X	X		X	
X		X	X	X	X	
X	X	X				
X		X	X	X		
		X	X	X		
	X	X		X		X
X		X	X			
		X				
X	X	X	X			
		X				
X		X	X	X	X	
X	X	X	X	X	X	X
		X	X	X		
X	X		X		X	X
X	X	X	X	X		
X		X	X	X	X	
	X	X	X	X		X
X	X	X	X	X		X
		X	X	X		
	X		X			X

	PAGE NUMBER	30 MINUTES OR LESS	MAKE-AHEAD	FREEZER FRIENDLY	LUNCHBOX FRIENDLY	VEGAN/ VEGETARIAN
Salmon and Egg Fried Rice	85	x	x			
Garlic Butter Shrimp Spaghetti and Steam-Roasted Green Beans	86	x				
Oven-Baked Cod and Asparagus with Garlic Buttered Toast	89	x				
Creamy Ricotta and Pea Pasta	90	x				x
Lentil and Spinach Dahl with Naan	93	x	x	x		x
Avocado, Black Bean and Mozzarella Quesadillas	94	x				x
Orange and Strawberry Sheet-Pan Pancakes	99	x	x	x	x	x
Chunky Chicken Soup	100		x	x		
Steak and Potato Dinner Hash	103					
Sheet-Pan Chicken Fajitas	104	x				
Baby-Friendly Buddha Bowl	107					x
Cheesy Beef Taco Pasta	108					
Mexican Chicken and Rice	111		x	x		
Chicken Chow Mein	115	x				
Sheet-Pan Mediterranean Salmon	116					
Carrot Cake Steel-Cut Oatmeal	121	x	x	x		x
Minestrone Soup	122					x
Baby-Friendly Chicken Curry	125		x	x		
Sweet Potato and Three-Bean Chili	128		x	x		x
Chicken and Barley Casserole	131		x	x		
Big-Flavor Cinnamon Applesauce	134	x	x	x		x
Shredded Beef Brisket	137		x	x		
Chicken, Mushroom and Pea Risotto	139					
Lentil Bolognese	143		x	x		x
Moroccan Lamb Stew	144		x	x		

DAIRY FREE	EGG FREE	NUT FREE	SOURCE OF IRON	SOURCE OF PROTEIN	SOURCE OF FIBER	MESSY MEAL
X		X	X	X		X
	X	X	X	X		
	X	X	X	X		
	X	X	X	X		X
		X	X	X	X	X
	X	X	X	X	X	
		X				
X	X	X	X	X		X
X	X	X	X	X		
X	X	X	X	X		
X	X	X	X	X	X	
		X	X	X		X
X	X	X	X	X		
X		X	X	X		
X	X	X	X			
X	X	X	X		X	X
X	X	X	X	X	X	X
X	X		X	X		X
X	X	X	X	X	X	X
X	X	X	X	X	X	X
X	X	X			X	X
		X	X	X		
	X	X	X	X		X
X	X	X	X	X	X	X
X	X	X	X	X		X

Acknowledgments

First and foremost, I would like to thank Sarah Monroe at Page Street Publishing, who reached out to me to make this book and helped me bring my vision to life. Your kindness, knowledge and expertise have made this process such a wonderful experience.

Dean Parry, my biggest cheerleader! Thank you for your unwavering support, for sacrificing so much of your time and for always believing in me. You proofread every last word of this book, and I will be forever grateful for your input.

Renae D'Andrea, thank you for agreeing to support me on this venture and for your invaluable contributions and expertise. As soon as it was decided that I would be writing a BLW cookbook, I knew you were the RDN I wanted to work with. I have so much respect for you and your work.

To my supporters at Zayne's Plate, it is because of you that I love what I do and have been able to embark on a career doing something I truly love. Knowing that your families enjoy my recipes means the world to me. Thank you for all of your support—this book is for you!

About the Author

Simone Ward is a mom of four and the creator of Zayne's Plate, a popular baby and toddler feeding Instagram blog that helps parents feed their families a wide variety of easy, healthy and tasty meals. With extensive experience in feeding babies, toddlers and children, Simone currently works in recipe development, creating nutritious, family-friendly food for clients both domestically and internationally.

Simone's work has been featured on various websites, including POPSUGAR's "20 Moms to Follow on Instagram For Major Lunchbox Inspiration," which highlighted Simone's flair and passion for creating fun and nutritious packed school lunches that kids love.

Index